Short Pieces
from
The
New
Dramatists

SHORT PIECES FROM THE NEW DRAMATISTS

First printing: May 1985
Second printing: June 1987

ISBN: 0-88145-029-4

Design by Marie Donovan
Set in Baskerville by L&F Technical Composition, Lakeland, FL
Printed and bound by The Whitlock Press, Middletown, NY

This Anthology Was Edited by

STAN CHERVIN

44 on 44th, by the Member Playwrights of New Dramatists, was originally performed on 19–22 January 1984 at New Dramatists, 424 West 44th Street, New York, NY 10036 under the direction of Susan Gregg, with the following Company:

Paul Collins	Anna Minot
Rodney Hudson	Michael Morin
Kathryn Hunter	Susan Pellegrino
Maria Maxwell	Leon Russom

Mary Errlinger was the Piano Player; Carol Klein, the Stage Manager; and David Milligan, the Technical Director.

Staff: Thomas G. Dunn, Director
Administration: Laurie Sammeth, General Manager; Heidi Edwards, Assistant to the Director; Elana Greenfield, Receptionist; Frank Va Vosa, Superintendent
Workshop Program: Casey Childs, Director; Rebecca Harrison, Associate
Artist Services: Stan Chervin, Director; Philip Bosakowski, Education Coordinator
Literary Services: Susan Gregg, Director; Michael Goodell, Assistant
Interns: Brook Berger, Ellen Blaufox, Sherrylynn L. Burney, Bill Cotter, Hank Krisch, Richard Le Comte, Joanne McEntyre, David Milligan

State of the Union, an evening of short plays by the member playwrights of New Dramatists, was originally performed on 23–27 January 1985 at New Dramatists, 424 West 44th Street, New York, NY 10036. The following members of the New Dramatists Director Unit directed the Company:

Alma Becker
Bob Engels
Thomas Gruenewald
John Pynchon Holms
Gideon Y. Schein

Page Burkholder
Rhea Gaisner
Bob Hall
Robert Moss

The Company:

Reg E. Cathey
Lisa Goodman
Anna Minot
Leon Russom

Paul Collins
Hazel J. Medina
Erika Petersen
Peter Zapp

Casey Childs was the Producer; Alma Becker, the Production Director; Robert DiMatteo, the Arranger/Pianist; David A. Milligan, the Production Manager; Sherrylynn Burney and Paul Bernstein, the Stage Managers; Susi Levi, the Assistant Stage Manager; and Tim Maner, the Assistant to Mr. Moss.

CONTENTS

Foreword   *Robert Anderson* .... *vii*
What Is New Dramatists? .... *ix*
How Did It All Begin?   *Michaela O'Harra* .... *xi*

Steve Carter
  Mirage 1
  The Inaugural Tea 4

Laura Cunningham
  The Rub 9
  Victims' Lunch 12

Gus Edwards
  Black is Black 19
  New Ice Age 22

Laura Harrington
  The Wrong Man 25

Jack Heifner
  Brilliants 31
  Pollster 35

Sherry Kramer
  Hold for Three 39

Romulus Linney
  Martha Miller 45
  Swans 47

Peter Maloney
  Between the Acts 53

Dennis McIntyre
The Boyfriend 59

Eric Overmyer
Hawker 63

Mac Wellman
No Smoking Piece 69
The Porcupine Man (*Music by Michael S. Roth*) 72

August Wilson
The Janitor 81

Dick D. Zigun
The Three-minute Manifesto for an
Uncle Sam on Stilts 85
Untimely Death with Dogs in Detail 88

FOREWORD

We were an innocent but heady group of New Dramatists that thirty-five years ago climbed to the top of Lindsay and Crouse's Hudson Theatre on West 44th Street week after week to listen to the likes of Maxwell Anderson, Elia Kazan, Robert Sherwood, Elmer Rice, S.N. Behrman, and Joshua Logan talk about playwriting and theatre. Our group of wide-eyed neophytes sitting in the shadows around the long boardroom table included Bill Inge, Paddy Chayefsky, Bill Gibson, Horton Foote, Joseph Hayes, Joe Kramm, Ronald Alexander, and Sumner Locke Elliot among others who, in due time, would themselves return to talk to new generations of New Dramatists including James Goldman, Michael Stewart, Max Wilk, Joe Masteroff, Arnold Schulman, Jack Gelber, John Guare, Rochelle Owens, Oliver Hailey, James Baldwin, and Megan Terry, who would in due time . . .

The 1985 crop of New Dramatists is much more sophisticated than we were in 1949. Though many of us had had options for Broadway productions, few of us had ever been produced anywhere or even heard our words read aloud. The present group has had plays produced all over the country at such prestigious theatres as The O'Neill Theatre Center, The Actors Theatre in Louisville, Arena Stage in Washington, La Mama, The Negro Ensemble Theatre, and St. Clements. They also have won innumerable grants, fellowships, and awards.

Still they come to The New Dramatists to go on with the learning process we all continue all our writing lives. And they honor The New Dramatists by their presence.

I believe it was Lope de Vega (who wrote over two thousand plays!) who said, "All you need for a theatre is two planks and a passion." Over the years The New Dramatists has provided the planks; the playwrights have provided the passion. It has been quipped that young poets are eighteen, young novelists, twenty-five, and young playwrights, thirty-six. I believe it is granted that playwriting is the most difficult form of writing because it is not just writing. It is learning that what is written on the page is only a blueprint. It is learning how to work with and through our valued collaborators, the director and the actors, to reach that mysterious mass of people, the audience, who sit there with what Brooks Atkinson called their "idiot genius."

At one time it was estimated that it takes ten years for a playwright to develop from a recognized talent to an actively producing playwright. The New Dramatists may not be able to hasten the process, but it can help to make it a time of meaningful growth, a shared experience among peers.

ROBERT ANDERSON

What Is New Dramatists?

New Dramatists has encouraged and developed playwriting talent in America since 1949. Though the theatre has changed considerably over the years since then, the need for New Dramatists is, if anything, greater than when the organization was founded. The theatre's demand for substantial new work continues to grow, and yet talent, education, ambition, and dreams make up only part of what writers need for successful careers in the theatrical profession. The rest of it —the opportunity for playwrights to explore the "how" of their art—is what New Dramatists provides.

New Dramatists offers its members a varied development program. Script-in-hand readings followed by panel discussions of the plays, writers' studios, free theatre tickets, a national script distribution service, a newsletter, a comprehensive theatre library, a loan fund, exchanges, and the chance to work with actors and directors unburdened by the pressures of publicity or production deadlines—these are our tangible services. The intangibles? Encouragement, support, membership in a community of gifted writers in a wide range of styles, and (perhaps most important) belief in the process.

In the midst of hundreds of producing theatres in the United States, ranging from Broadway through regional companies to alternative and experimental groups, New Dramatists remains unique. Producing *playwrights* rather than plays, it is a workshop in the purest sense of the word. We provide a place to work, a climate for inspiration, and the means and opportunities to realize aspiration.

New Dramatists charges its members neither dues nor fees, seeks no rights to its members' work, does not produce or license, and thus cannot hope for royalties or profits. The theatrical profession, a mixture of funding sources, and other interested friends contribute toward helping us continue our important work.

Over the past 36 years, New Dramatists has served over 500 playwrights. At present, there are 46 active members in the program.

How Did It All Begin?

By New Dramatists Founder Michaela O'Harra

With a gleam in its mother's eye—the gleam of a tear (of frustration, despair, and alas, self-pity). Why, with all the moaning about the lack of new playwrights, didn't somebody DO something?! Something to help bring to maturity the gifts of writers right under their noses, writers like me, and others whose work I knew through having been Mike Todd's story editor, having read for other producers, film companies, agents.

Each had proof of potential—options by noted producers and/or a professional production or two, many well received by critics out of or in New York itself. All of us were young, eager to learn what we knew we had to know—how to meet the special demands of the theatre and its large audiences. But how to get the kind of practical experience we needed NOW?! Where?!

Analyzing what had to be learned then, and how, I came to believe that through organized means, much of it could be provided now. A theatre-wide facility could be set up through which each element of the industry could channel its contributions towards the creation of a climate similar in a small way to theatre conditions years ago which encouraged writers for the stage. The playwriting gifts and skills of 15-30 demonstrably talented selectees could grow in a climate created by (1) much theatre-going made possible by producer-granted free admissions to all the plays done in New York; (2) informal roundtable craft discussions with established playwrights, producers, scene designers, actors whose work the group had seen; (3) production observance posts arranged for individuals so as to see how a play is sometimes improved, sometimes damaged by revisions between first reading and its opening in New York or failure out of town; (4) a workshop in which plays could be panel discussed, revised or not, then directed, rehearsed, and performed by professionals.

I wrote all this up in voluminous detail, gave it the grandiose title *A Plan For Playwrights*, proposed that the Dramatists Guild set up the facility to put the Plan's four projects into operation, calling on the entire theatre community for its self-interested participation. All very well, but who would pay attention to such a proposal dreamed up by a total nobody?

Then I remembered a Dramatists Guild meeting held in a huge theatre. The council sat at a table facing an audience of several hundred members, many of the most vocal and bitter playwrights, demanding that the Guild could do something to help them. The demands being taken by a lone, sandy-haired figure, standing at the foots, peering down through his glasses at the mob, understanding their hurt, despair, and bitterness, giving each speaker courteous, patient attention. Remembering, I thought "That's my man. Howard Lindsay," and sent him my proposal.

Upon meeting, he said "My God, girl—I admire your thinking, your ambition, but this is utterly impossible. I'd be willing to meet, talk with a small group, even get others to do it, encourage them to stick to their typewriters but—that's about all you can hope for." He shook his head, asked nitty-gritty rhetorical questions like "Have you any idea what this would cost?" and "How in hell could we select 15–30 writers, discriminate among the hundreds of Guild members?"

I took a deep breath and quoted facts I'd collected about possible sources of support: The Playwrights Company hadn't given its $3,000 award to the most promising playwright of the season for the past two years. Katharine Cornell had a theatre foundation. John Golden was always generous with new playwrights. As for selections—the theatre industry itself was already a committee at large. I had devised a point system with the playwright applicant winning the most telling points for options and productions, others for recommendations from established agents, producers, directors, and for grants from foundations relying on theatre people as judges.

At last he suggested I make up a twelve-member group of the kind of writers I was talking about. He would have us see Life With Mother. He and Russel Crouse would meet with us, hear how we explained its being less successful than *Life With Father*.

The participants in that meeting so impressed him that he at once began the exercise of his prestige and power on behalf of my plan. Within a few weeks we had that $6,000 from The Playwrights Company; its members Robert Sherwood, Maxwell Anderson, S. N. Behrman, Elmer Rice, and John Wharton, together with Richard Rodgers and Oscar Hammerstein, and Moss Hart as president of The Dramatists Guild had joined us in forming The New Dramatists' first board of directors. We also had our first office, a tiny cubbyhole under the stairs of the Hudson Theatre, owned by Lindsay and Crouse. And we were "in business."

STEVE CARTER was the recipient of a 1982 Guggenheim Award and has been both Playwright-in-residence and Director of the Playwright's Workshop at New York's Negro Ensemble Company. His plays *Terraces, Eden,* and *Nevis Mountain Dew* received their world premieres there, and *Eden* was subsequently staged in Chicago, Cleveland, London, and Los Angeles. The play was published by Samuel French and won a Distinguished Playwriting Award from the Los Angeles Drama Critics Circle. *Nevis Mountain Dew* has been produced at Arena Stage and in Chicago. It is published by Dramatists Play Service and was included in the 1978–1979 Burns Mantle Yearbook as one of that season's Ten Best Plays. Mr. Carter has received both a National Endowment for the Arts Creative Writing Fellowship and a Rockefeller Foundation Fellowship. His plays *Dame Lorraine* and *Shadows* premiered at Chicago's Victory Gardens Theatre where he was the first playwright-in-residence, director of playwrights' workshops, and literary manager, and is now a special consultant. He recently returned from Marin County, California, where he was a guest artist and faculty member at the Bay Area Playwrights Festival VII for which he wrote a short play, *Primary Colors.* He is currently writing a screenplay for a film based on his two plays *One Last Look* and *Eden* for Tobias Productions. He was elected to membership in New Dramatists in 1981.

MIRAGE

Steve Carter

Characters

WOMAN
MAN

(*A female burglar enters an apartment via its fire escape window and ransacks the place, looking for small and portable items. Hearing keys at the door, she hides in a closet. A man enters, sees the condition of the place, and picks up the phone.*)

MAN: Hello, Police? I've been robbed. Come over! I've been robbed. What do you mean, "calm down!"? I've been robbed! No! No! My apartment. Okay! Okay! Burglarized, then. What difference does it make? My address is two twenty . . . What? I have to come over there? Don't you even want to dust for fingerprints or whatever it is you do? Hello? Hello? Well, I'll be damned!

WOMAN: Okay, Mack. Freeze!

MAN: I'll be damned!

WOMAN: Probably . . . if you don't get those hands up, Bosco!

MAN: But . . . you're a woman.

WOMAN: Wanna make something of it, Mandrake?

MAN: Women don't rob . . . er . . . burgle apartments.

WOMAN: It's a new day, Buster!

MAN: I don't believe this!

WOMAN: (*Motioning with a gun.*) Believe this, Jocko!

MAN: I'll not be intimidated by a woman.

WOMAN: (*Indicating gun.*) Then be intimidated by this, Buddy.

MAN: But . . . I'm a man.

WOMAN: Does that necessarily mean you have to be stupid, Booby?

MAN: What is it you want? I don't have much.

WOMAN: Not from where I'm standing, Lover.

MAN: I have a television. Take it and get out!

WOMAN: Nineteen inches? You're bigger than that, I'll bet, Pet. Ain't you got no "State of the Art" stuff, MacDuff?

MAN: No!

WOMAN: You know, I don't like your tone or your 'tude. Same old double standard shit, again. 'Cause I'm a woman, you ain't scared enough, right? You think I won't really use this. (*She puts gun to his head.*) Hah! Ready to pee in your pants now? Betcha you're thinking, "This bitch is really gonna kill me. If I had that gun, I'd show her a thing or three." eh, Butch?

MAN: Please. This has gone far enough. Please go and I won't say anything.

WOMAN: Shut up, Louie!

(*She whacks him with the gun. He sprawls.*)

WOMAN: Galls you, don't it, Laddie Bucko. A fine broth of boy like you being laid low by a mere slip of a lass, Ass

MAN: Don't . . .

WOMAN: Don't hurt you? Are you begging this "woman" for mercy, Percy?

MAN: Please . . .

WOMAN: Say your Act of Contrition, Dude.

MAN: No! Please . . . listen . . .

WOMAN: Strip, Pip!

MAN: What?

WOMAN: Strip! Outta the duds! Off mit der hosen, Rosen!

MAN: I beg your pardon . . .

WOMAN: I beg your hardon. Didn't think I was going to pass this up, did you, Liebling?

MAN: But this is . . .

WOMAN: Right, Termite! A little trick we learned from you guys. It's called Rape, Ape!

MAN: But, I can't . . .

WOMAN: It's either that or you get it right where the Monogahela and the Allegheny meet to form the Ohio, Chico!

MAN: Pittsburgh?

WOMAN: Right in the mills, Baby Doll! See how you like it when the shoe's on the other foot. Take it off! Take it all off, Orloff!

(She threatens to whack him again. He strips down to his skivvies as she hums, "The Stripper.")

WOMAN: Man. You ain't half bad, Dad. Sorry I gotta tie your hands. Don't want you trying no Boy Scout shit to ruin my fun. 'Sides, you won't be needing your hands. Won't gag you though. You're gonna need your mouth. If you get my drift. Plus . . . I want you to tell me you love what I'm doing and how I'm the best and all that . . . Don't tell me I ain't an incurable romantic! See? I even turn the lights out for some atmosphere. Now, Sport, to work! Ooh . . . there's more to you than meats the eye. Get it? More to you than M-E-A-T-S the eye. Get to it, Macho-Man! Mama let you live a little longer, you do it right.

(Grunts, groans, and stuff. The gun goes off. The lights come on.)

MAN: Wow! What a fuckin' turn-on! Your dad told me I'd not ever regret the day I married you.

WOMAN: Your dad told me the same thing. What've you planned for tomorrow?

MAN: And spoil the surprise?

BLACKOUT

TEA ON INAUGURATION DAY

Steve Carter

OLD WOMAN: Got this friend. Should say, "I had this friend." Anyway . . . been friends since childhood. Could be sisters, we so much alike. Always like the same things. Same food. Same clothes. Same men . . . when we were young enough to do something 'bout it. Always like the same things. Even vote alike. Believe me, we seen a few presidents come and go. Lord . . . Didn't think we had the strength to go on when the ol' man die. Didn't like the idea of him cheatin' on ol' Eleanor. She weren't much to look at, that's true . . . but she was a carin' woman. However, he did have a hard life . . . bein' cripple and all. Maybe it was good he had a little forbidden fruit 'fore he left this earth. Always wondered how he did it with them braces and crutches. Then there was my Jack. Now, I never did care for his wife, but I loved that man . . . and my friend did, too. Anyway, she suppose to come over here today for tea. Both of us had this 'greement that if this one got back in the White House for four more years, we would both have tea and put poison in it and just check on outta here!

I can't stand him! Never was so good a actor 'till he start to mess with politics. I 'member him in the movies. Only two times I ever enjoy myself at one o' his flicks. First was when they cut off his legs in that picture where he was in love with Robert Cummings or somebody. Played that role and see how his son turn out? Pictures know, child! Pictures know! Second time was when he played in "The Killers." No, child. The remake! The remake! That's where he showed his true colors. Played the villain. He ordered the killing . . . just like he doin' now. Now he got four more years . . . and get in by a landslide . . . he gonna really show his behind. Don't give a damn 'bout nobody 'cept his rich friends. Every time I get ready to watch some of my programs on the teevee, here he come with some damn news conference.

Then they got to hold up the program even more while some fool explain what he say. He don't mean nobody no good. Look how he call up that man with the fake heart and cause him to have a stroke 'cause he told him he was going to cut his Social Security. Had to flip-flop next day in the papers, but I betcha the man don't get his check. Oh, I was so glad they cut his legs off in "King's Row." Everytime it come on teevee, that's the only part I watch. If they had gone ahead and give him the 'cademy award for it, I might not be havin' this problem today. Anyway, my friend call me up and tell me . . . after she vote and all . . . she tell me she get in the booth and somethin' tell her to change her mind and vote for "him." Could hardly believe my ears. She say all of a sudden she start thinkin' 'bout what could happen if Mondale die or get bump off. She don't trust no woman bein' in charge of nothin' 'cause they too irrational. Can't argue with her there, 'cause she done prove her point when she change her vote! Plus, she say that would mean the Mafia be in control of the country. I had to remind her that even though my Jack was Catholic, the Pope didn't take over then . . . even 'though it look like he tryin' now . . . don't it? She come tellin' me the Mafia and Pope ain't the same. Know what I told her? I told her, "Hah!" Then she come tellin' me how Mondale don't look right. He do have this gangster face, I have to admit. Never will understand why when he had that little piece o' stuff done on his face, he didn't have his nose straightened all the way and did something 'bout that luggage he carrying under his eyes. She ain't entirely wrong when she say he don't look as healthy as this other one. I really ain't never seen Mondale doin' nothin' manly. This one always ridin' a horse or choppin' wood or pullin' in his stomach and stridin' like he a general or somethin' whenever he even see somebody with a movie camera. No wonder he fall 'sleep whenever he can. Did see Mondale in the rain, though. Cowboy and his lady don't never go out in the rain 'cause they 'fraid all that hair dye run down and turn the grass black and yellow. And speakin' o' that article, you see her lately? She ain't got much longer, I tell you! Ain't got no shoulders. Go straight

from her neck to her waist. Straight up and down like six
o'clock. Somethin' inside her havin' a good meal. Talk
'bout a woman being in charge. I told my friend that there's
one in charge right now . . . 'cause she tell that fool the
answer to all the questions . . . 'cause he can't hear
'em . . . even when he 'wake. I don't believe he was even
shot that time. He just tryin' to look good to the
people . . . like he some God . . . and can't die. Shoot, he
ain't even show off his scars like Lyndon.

Then my friend come tellin' me she had a suspicion he
was gonna win and she like to be on the winnin' side. I told
her behine she black. She ain't never been on the winnin'
side. Fool didn't want the black vote. He ain't go out and
seek it. When last you hear tell of that? Sure knew how to
grab them Pritty Ricans though. Put a few o' them in some
little ass positions and got them thinking they white and
American. Well, they ain't like bein' lump with us no how.
Winnin' side? Hah! Honey, we ain't nothin' in this country
now. Plus, she old. Old people ain't had no business votin'
for that man. Lord, I bet he ain't nothin' but tubes and her-
nia 'neath them suits o' his. Well, I told her I ain't servin'
her no poison tea 'cause I want her to live to regret what she
done. I know I ain't drinkin' no poison-up tea 'cause I want
to be here and see her regret what she done. I'm gonna tell
her, "I told you so!" Everybody going to be sorry, believe
me. Thought Hitler was bad? Hah! You ain't seen nothin'
yet. Well, let me go watch my favorite movie on my VCR.
"Casablanca"! It's my favorite 'cause he wasn't in it. He
almost was, though. Can you see him instead of ol' Bogey?
Yeah, he was almost in it, but them Warner Brothers knew
something Annenberg and Gimbel didn't. See ya'll!

CURTAIN

LAURA CUNNINGHAM was born and raised in New York. She is the author of two published novels, *Third Parties* and *Sweet Nothings* (excerpted in the *Atlantic Monthly*). She has published hundreds of stories and articles in such publications as *The Atlantic, Esquire, Newsday, Mademoiselle, Vogue,* the *Chicago Tribune,* and the New York *Times.* She served a three-month stint at the New York *Times,* writing the "Hers" column, and has often contributed essays and articles to that newspaper. Her work has been widely reprinted and anthologized. She is the author of three plays, *Beautiful Bodies* (nominated for the 1983 National Play Award), *Bang,* and *Cruisin' Close To Crazy.* Her works have been given staged readings at Playwrights Horizons, Ensemble Studio Theatre, the Actor's Theatre of Louisville, and other regional theatres. She is currently at work on a fourth play and a third novel.

THE RUB

Laura Cunningham

Cast

Attractive WOMAN (late twenties)
Attractive MAN (early twenties)

(*Scene: The bedroom of a young woman's apartment.* WOMAN *is kneeling on the bed, alongside the prone body of a young* MAN. *She dreamily applies body lotion to his bare back.*)

WOMAN: That's a great muscle. I've never seen a back this . . . (*She searches for the word.*) delineated. (*Catching herself*) not that I've seen that many backs. Only a few. But this one is really special.

MAN: (*Voice muffled in bedding.*) I work out on Nautilus.

WOMAN: I bet you get sore. (*Applying more massage cream.*) Relax. Your arms will be better at your sides. One second. (*She runs her own hands together.*) I'm warming the lotion in my hands. Cold lotion can be . . . such a shock. (*Gently rubbing cream on his skin.*) Ummm . . . I'm having trouble deciding . . . which is my favorite section. Your neck is . . . sweet. What an innocent little neck.

MAN: (*Cutting in flat.*) My latissimus dorsi. Most girls like my latissimus dorsi.

WOMAN: (*To disguise her ignorance of the muscle groups.*) Oh, the dorsi! (*Pause*) They're nice. They're nice, too. But I'm more drawn to your shoulders. They look like they could . . . I don't know . . . shoulder a lot. (*She continues, rubbing more intensely.*) I bet you could even run, carrying someone on your shoulders . . . (*Pause*) Your skin has the most amazing texture. Sort of . . . pebbly. Like stucco. (*Pause*) Am I touching you with just the right amount of pressure? How's this?

MAN: More to the right.

WOMAN: Between the shoulder blades? Is this it? Is this the spot? Is this where you hurt?

MAN: Almost. Just a smidge more to the right.

WOMAN: Right.

MAN: (*Inarticulate sounds of pain, pleasure.*) Oh . . . oh . . . yeah . . . uh . . . uh . . .

WOMAN: I'll just keep doing this, then. Up and down, round and round. Up and down, round and round. Do you know you're always supposed to rub in the direction of the heart? Oh, yes. Everything I've done is toward your heart. Okay, are you ready? Here's the grand finale. From the tips of your toes . . . (*Pause, as she studies the toe.*) Oh, this is a funny little toesy. It's sort of . . . permanently curled.

MAN: Prehensile. I have prehensile use of my toes. I can pull light cords. Sometimes, I can even write.

WOMAN: God, that's amazing. *You're* amazing. We're going to find out so many wonderful little things about each other . . . (*Pause, ecstatic tone*) I wouldn't have *believed* it could be this . . . (*She searches for the word.*) simple. Just so simple and natural. I almost didn't go out tonight . . . But something made me. And there you were and (*Sigh*) here we are. We're so lucky. Most people wander around all their lives and never find this . . . You know, even if the worst thing could happen, happened . . . now. I wouldn't care. Oh, I would care . . . if I were blown up, or something . . . but as long as we're together, it doesn't scare me. Isn't it a miracle? It takes only one other person, one other person, to keep away the dark. (*Soft, reverent*) To make dreams come true, to honor the great trust. Fell. Between us. This is the only warm place in the city tonight, the only warm place in the world . . .

(MAN *starts to ease out of her embrace, and rises from the bed.*)

WOMAN: Isn't it? Sweetie? What is it? Can I get you something? More wine? A soda? (*She rises, dragging blanket.*)

MAN: It's late.

(WOMAN *comprehends—he is leaving. She stops in her tracks.*)

MAN: I'll call.

WOMAN: Call? Call!

(*A beat, low.*)

WOMAN: Don't bother. (*She spins away, muttering to herself.*)
Oh, boy. I sensed it. I sensed it all along. I kept denying it.
Thinking, "benefit of the doubt, benefit of the doubt" but
the warnings were registering all along. That wild light in
your left eye. Okay, "eyes of blue" but a white streak in one
eye is strictly weirdo. Siberian husky. And the curling toes?
Who ever saw that?

MAN: I can't get behind your sarcasm.

WOMAN: (*Low but angered.*) Then get in front of it. "Behind
my sarcasm." What an original way to put it. What use of
language. Why didn't you say so sooner? You could have
saved me the trouble . . .

MAN: It's late.

WOMAN: You want to go, so go.

MAN: (*Dresses to leave.*) No.

WOMAN: I said "Go."

MAN: I can't find my other glove.

WOMAN: I saw something there, on the chair.

(MAN *retrieves glove, turns awkwardly before exiting.*)

MAN: Well, so long.

(WOMAN *turns away, flinches as door shuts. She stands alone on
stage, holding bottle of massage cream.*)

WOMAN: (*Soft, ironic*) Who needs you?

LIGHTS FADE

CURTAIN

THE VICTIMS' LUNCH

Laura Cunningham

Cast

YOUNG MAN
OLDER MAN
SECOND YOUNG MAN
LIONEL MARTIN
LINDA

(*A stark luncheon hall. A* YOUNG MAN *walks across stage, pauses, as if clearing his throat before a microphone. Microphone shrieks.* WOMAN, OLDER MAN, SECOND YOUNG MAN *enter, face him, as if attending a luncheon meeting.*)

YOUNG MAN: Welcome to the forty-third meeting of the Victims' Lunch Society. (*Pause*) Next Sunday's meeting will be cancelled, as it falls on a religious holiday.

OLDER MAN: What holiday?

SECOND YOUNG MAN: (*Hushing him.*) Sssssh.

YOUNG MAN: Our secretary, Linda, was scheduled to read the minutes of our last meeting, but I see Linda has not arrived yet . . .

SECOND YOUNG MAN: (*Querulous tone*) It's strange. She's never late.

OLDER MAN: She may be having flashbacks. Ever since the second mugging . . . She's just not herself.

YOUNG MAN: (*Whining, cutting him off.*) Well, whatever, Linda's not here, and we're a bit short for time today as our guest speaker has to catch a plane to Chicago . . . (*He checks his watch.*) . . . at one forty-five.

OLDER MAN: What? He knew it was a lunch. He couldn't leave more time. It's not as if we spent more than our budget to pay him to be here.

YOUNG MAN: We're lucky to have him, he's in demand. His book has been on the bestseller list for ten weeks. He's just managed to squeeze us in to his busy schedule.

OLDER MAN: That was big of him.

YOUNG MAN: (*Embarrassed, clearing his throat.*) Please let's use the time we *do* have. I'm happy to present our guest speaker, Lionel Martin, the author of the bestselling "VICTIM-OLOGY: ARE YOU BORN TO LOSE?"

(LIONEL MARTIN, *a celebrity lecturer: handsome, smug, appears, looking at his watch whenever possible.*)

SECOND YOUNG MAN: What about the minutes? You didn't read the minutes from last week?

OLDER MAN: I thought we were going to eat before the speech?

YOUNG MAN: (*Becoming harassed*) All right . . . all right. I'll read the minutes. You can all start on the fruit cup.

(YOUNG MAN *motions to* LIONEL MARTIN: *Wait. This will be a minute.* LIONEL MARTIN *looks annoyed.*)

OLDER MAN: Excuse me, but I believe, I requested, last time, instead of the fruit cup, if I could have a simple green salad? I'm allergic.

YOUNG MAN: (*More harried*) I asked the caterer . . . (*He looks around.*) Where is that waiter? I specifically asked him for one green salad.

OLDER MAN: Never mind. I knew I wouldn't get it.

YOUNG MAN: (*Reading minutes*) "At the August 30th meeting, we welcomed John Harding, who gave a moving account of how he was mugged in the doorway of his building, his fur coat taken, a gold chain ripped from around his throat . . .

(SECOND YOUNG MAN *stands, in acknowledgment.*)

YOUNG MAN: Ken Upjohn . . .

(OLDER MAN *stands briefly, in acknowledgment.*)

YOUNG MAN: Ken Upjohn gave a report on his litigation against the Board of Education, claiming his kindergarten class was left unguarded and he was terrorized by extremely large sixth graders . . .

OLDER MAN: They were giants! In the sixth grade: They were fourteen. They shave!

YOUNG MAN: Linda Burk described her first sexual assault in detail for the benefit of our new members . . .

(LINDA *enters, rushed, breathless. She has a distracted manner, and nonstop delivery. She speaks urgently, but without animation.*)

LINDA: I'm sorry. I know I'm late. I couldn't get a cab and so I ran all the way here . . . Finally, I got on a bus, and *it* stalled. So I ran down the subway, even though I hate them, and then I started feeling . . . you know . . . my claustrophobia. There was this awful man . . . He could have sat down, but he stood . . . right over me, and kept fooling with something under his coat. He had big bug eyes, and he kept looking at me, like I dare you. . . . All of a sudden, I thought, if I don't get off at the next stop, I'm going to expire. . . .

YOUNG MAN: (*Cutting her short.*) Linda . . . Linda . . . That's all right. We've had to start without you because we have a guest speaker today, Mr. Lionel Martin, whose time is extremely limited . . .

(LINDA *takes her seat.*)

LINDA: Oh, I'm sorry, I'm sorry. I didn't realize. . . .

YOUNG MAN: Well, that's all right but we must move along. I would like to introduce Lionel Martin. . . . Please give him a hand . . .

(*There is a smattering of applause.*)

YOUNG MAN: Lionel Martin is one of the few victimologists in the United States, and he is honoring us with his presence today, as he has a scheduled TV appearance in Chicago . . .

LIONEL MARTIN: (*Self-centered, but with flashes of charm.*) I have to be at JFK at one forty-five, which means: You better kick me out in about . . . (*He checks watch.*) ten minutes. (*He notices food is being served.*) Please enjoy your meal. What I have to say won't take long . . .

YOUNG MAN: Those of you who ordered the Chicken á la king, please signal the waiter by turning your coffee cup upside down . . . If you are having ribs au jus . . . just raise your right hand as the waiter approaches your table.

(*Hands are raised.*)

LIONEL MARTIN: My premise is simple—even morons could understand it. Why are some people the victims of violent crime? (*He looks at* LINDA.) Often repeatedly, while others . . . (*He touches his vest, meaning himself.*) go through their entire lives without suffering a single incident? Is it possible that there is some inner mechanism that signals potential attackers, that some people are victims and others are not?

OLDER MAN: This isn't chicken . . . It's some kind of soy chunks.

LINDA: Oh, it's all that microwaved shit.

YOUNG MAN: I beg to dicker . . . (*Catching slip of tongue.*) *differ* with you. The whole point of our organization is victims' rights. (*Highest whine*) Why are we abused? Why is there no recourse? (*Hurt*) I thought you would offer us some positive advice. We try to be . . . uh . . . positive all the time.

LIONEL MARTIN: There may be some attitudes—in posture, dress, manner of walking, choice of occupation and address . . . all subconscious signals to the criminal. You may well be inviting him: "Mug me! Rape me! Rob me!"

LINDA: (*Outraged*) "Rape me!?" (*To* YOUNG MAN) Why did you invite him? Did you know this was his attitude?

LIONEL MARTIN: (*To* LINDA) Well, and I only use you as an example: Look at your suggestive, see-through blouse. (*He peers lasciviously at* LINDA.)

LINDA: See-through! Man, you have X-ray eyes!

LIONEL MARTIN: Your very breathlessness, your walk, the bounce of your . . . uh . . . parts, are all possibly contributing factors in your *how many* rapes?

LINDA: Two, and it's none of your business! I have a right to bounce.

OLDER MAN: She was attacked in her own apartment: A man climbed through a vent!

LIONEL MARTIN: Twice? (*To* SECOND YOUNG MAN) And you? Why were you wearing a fur coat and gold chains? Weren't you flashing for some criminal? Didn't you *all,* when you think back on it, in some way, ask for it?

SECOND YOUNG MAN: No!

OLDER MAN: Never! Who asked you here!

YOUNG MAN: We were victims!

LIONEL MARTIN: That's my point. Psychologically, you always set yourself up for pain, failure, humiliation. . . .

(*They rise, en masse.*)

YOUNG MAN: (*Signalling the others.*) Kill!

(*The victims overpower the speaker, chasing him from the stage.*)

OLDER MAN: (*Final whine*) No dessert?

BLACK OUT

CURTAIN

GUS EDWARDS was born in Antigua and has lived in the United States since he was eighteen. In 1977 the O'Neill Conference read his *Black Body Blues* as a TV project. Later that year, the Negro Ensemble Company produced his play *The Offering*. Since that time they've produced three others: *Black Body Blues* (1978), *Old Phantoms* (1979), and *Weep Not For Me* (1981). Other productions include the American Premiere Stage's presentation of his short plays: *Three Fallen Angels* and *The Candidate's Been Shot*. *The Offering* and *Old Phantoms* have been published by Dramatists Play Service, and *Three Fallen Angels* is included in the anthology *Center Stage*, published earlier this year. Mr. Edwards received a Rockefeller Playwrights grant in 1979, the same year he became a New Dramatist. His most recent play *Manhattan Made Me* was presented at The Negro Ensemble Company in the Spring of 1983.

BLACK IS BLACK

Gus Edwards

Cast

A black man (any age)

Setting

Anywhere (may be a park with a bench)

MAN: You know, it's funny, but when you talk about the situation of being black in America, white people who don't know better will tell you that you are being oversensitive —being paranoid . . . But the truth is that they would have to get into a black man's skin just one time and then they wouldn't say that no more . . .

Give you an example: Any black man with sense knows, that if you ever get stopped by a cop—no matter for what bullshit reason he stopping you—your best bet is to smile and answer the man, "Yes sir." "No sir." Because all that bastard want is for you to get smart and start acting hostile. Then he gon try to bust your head open with his club . . . Now if it turn out that you're innocent of whatever bullshit thing he stop you for in the first place, then he might plant some stuff on you and say it was a "drug bust." Who gon argue with him? . . . Man is a cop—and he's white. Right?

Now I'm going to tell you about some shit I seen that was goddamn unbelievable.

I was at a boxing match one night in Madison Square Garden. This is going back some years now. Muhammed Ali was on the bill. Now, nobody could bring the folks out like Ali. Every cat in New York was there—dressed up and glittering.

Now I'm in the place with my friend, Lucien. We save half a year to see this thing. Sitting damn near ringside.

Now down in front of us is a young black boy. And he seemed to be having a problem. The manager, a little bald man, ask him to show his ticket stub and my man refused, claiming that the cat at the door took it. Now that excuse is lame. Everybody knows that these rude black boys like to buy the cheapest seats for way up there and then sneak down to the more expensive ones at ringside.

But, the manager didn't argue. He just said "Okay" and left. My man laughed . . . a minute later the manager was back—with two white cops. The cops ask him to show his ticket, and my man told them to "Go to hell."—I was impressed. Takes a lot of heart to answer a cop like that, black or white. Cop asked him again—my man showed them his finger.—Now this is getting serious. Folks around even start offering advice. "Hey man, cool it. They got the badge and they got the gun. They also got the color. You know you can't win."

But my man gave them cops so much trouble that finally one said, "This is a waste of time," and went in to get him.

Well, the cop just about got in range when the black boy nailed him, a picture perfect uppercut, right on the button. It was a pretty thing to watch. (*He demonstrates it.*) The cop went flying over two rows of seats.

Now the other cop had his gun out and pointing it at my man. "Come the hell out here. And now! . . . " His voice was shaking but the gun was looking steady and mean.

My man had to go. We all shook our heads, because we knew that in a matter of minutes there was going to be one broken-up black boy and there was nothing anybody could do about it. Because, that's how it is. Mess with a cop, and you got it coming . . . (*Pause*) expecially a white one.

Now the fight was about the begin, and we don't forget all about this mess, when I heard some noise in the back. Looked around and it was my man coming down the aisle waving his hand like he was some kind of politician looking for votes. When he got closer I saw it was a ticket the cat was waving. A ringside ticket. People in our section gave him a big hand when he sat down—almost as big a hand as we gave Ali when he showed up.

Man, if you had bet me money that my man wouldn't have gotten away hitting a cop, you would've won all I had.

To this day, I don't know how he worked that one out.
It's a mystery to me. I saw it with my own eyes—and I still,
to tell you the truth, right to this moment—don't——

Lights

NEW ICE AGE

Gus Edwards

Cast

A derelict (black) wearing a tattered old raincoat, carrying a duffle bag. He is a man past fifty, but seems ageless.

Setting

A park bench isolated in a lighted area, surrounded by darkness. Maybe there is a garbage can nearby.

When the lights come up, the derelict wanders in with the duffle bag. He sits and shivers as a cold wind passes through him. He searches through the bag and finds an old scarf which he wraps around his neck.

DERELICT: Look at the sky and you can see the clouds turning cold. Wintertime in Harlem. Five o'clock in the afternoon and —darkness all around. The sun done called it a day, and there ain't no moon anybody can find . . . Alley cats peep out from where they been hiding, cop cars prowl the streets, and everybody heading home, like zombies, to get where it's warm.

I got no place to go. This here is my home. But that don't bother me. What does though—is how cold this place is getting to be. And I ain't talking about the weather . . . Seems to me we going through a New Ice Age where everything is cold, frozen, and dead.

Now it wasn't always like that. There used to be a time when these streets were warm, people was civil—and Harlem was a different place. A place where the living came to enjoy life.

You still hear the old music sometimes—see the old photographs, but it's gone. All gone. (*Music—from the period—fades in behind him, softly.*) The men in their zoot suits, women in them slinky dresses—gold teeth and flowers in their hair. Reefers, alcohol, hot music, and noise. And I was in the middle of most of it. Tuxedo suit, processed hair, and hip to all the new sliding dances . . . (*He rises, discards his raincoat, and moves forward, poised and transformed into what he used to be in the old day.*) A coffee-colored fox on his arm, and a brown-skinned mama on that.

"Move it baby! Strut! Strut!

I seen it all and more. Mixed with everybody. Stayed up till the moon went down and the sun came out shining. Drove around in fast cars, but somehow got left behind when the whole parade turned the corner . . . Why? . . . I don't know. Maybe I got too old.

Louis Armstrong, Billie Holliday, Ethel Waters, Duke Ellington, Bo Jangles, and all them others walked these streets and blessed this area with the music of their soul. This is a holy ground, if you know what I mean. This place should be a shrine to the talent and life that was spent here. Somebody should anoint it as the Blackman's Capital, the way Rome is for Catholics and DC is for the Nation, before this new cold spell passes and takes it all away. But what can you do? Maybe it's too late already . . . and who am I to be telling you what you should, and shouldn't, be doing? Just another dirty derelict, shuffling through the streets looking for a handout. Ain't that so?

Well, I ain't one to argue. After all, I still got my memories. What've you got?

Lights

For all rights other than stock and amateur production, please contact Mary Harden, Bret Adams Ltd., 448 West 44th Street, New York, NY 10036.

LAURA HARRINGTON's first screenplay, *The Listener*, was workshopped at the 1983 Eugene O'Neill Theater Conference. *Free Fall*, her first full-length stage play, has been staged and read at the Women's Project of the American Place Theater, the Douglas Fairbanks Theater, NYC, and Capital Repertory, Albany, NY. She was recently commissioned to write a one act for the Actors Theater of Louisville, *Women and Shoes*. *Cheat* has won the 1984 Hunter College One Act Playwriting Contest. *Cheat* was produced at the Emerson Main Stage in Boston for the 1984 One Act Play Festival of Playwright's Platform. Ms. Harrington received the Goodman Fund Grant from the City University of New York and was nominated for the Susan Smith Blackburn Award for *Free Fall*. She was guest artist-in-residence at Skidmore College during the 1984–85 school year. She is currently co-writing a documentary for the National Film Board of Canada, ALZHEIMER: UNE VUE D'HORREUR. She was elected to New Dramatists in 1984.

THE WRONG MAN

Laura Harrington

(*A party.* NADIA *is alone on the balcony, dancing.* JOHN *enters, watches* NADIA, *and begins dancing with her. She dances with him for a beat or two, then turns her back on him.*)

JOHN: Excuse me——

NADIA: (*Turning to face him.*) No . . . We're not going to do that.

JOHN: I just wanted to know——

NADIA:——My name.

JOHN: Right.

NADIA: I've done that before. You've done that before. Tonight we're going to do something new . . . Instead of the usual banalities we're going to lie to each other.

JOHN: Oh, sure.

NADIA: About the last time we met——

JOHN: What are you talking about?

NADIA: The last time we met. Which was the first time. That's where we start.

JOHN: The first time . . .?

NADIA: Before anything happened.

JOHN: (*Sarcastic*) Right. Before anything happened.

NADIA: You've go it now.

JOHN: You're serious about this.

NADIA: Very.

(*A beat.*)

JOHN: I'm not sure I know how to do this.

NADIA: It's easy. Believe me.

(*Pause*)

JOHN: Okay . . . Okay . . . It was a party . . .

NADIA: A dance.

JOHN: A party, a dance . . . You were dancing.

NADIA: I could feel you watching me.

JOHN: I had been watching you for a very long time.

NADIA: I was careful near you . . .

JOHN: A summer night.

NADIA: Late summer.

JOHN: You sat next to another girl who turned to you and said: "You're very beautiful" . . . and you laughed.

NADIA: I'd been drinking . . . it was a party . . .

JOHN: A dance.

NADIA: And I'd been dancing . . .

JOHN: You sat next to me. Very close. Your thigh lay pressed against mine . . . I felt that I could almost, not quite, touch your breast . . .

NADIA: I was heady with liquor, with the night, with the surprise of your heat, with this girl telling me I was beautiful . . . I looked up, you were reaching your arms out to pull me to my feet, and I thought . . . "He is going to pick me right up out of my skin."

JOHN: I'd never touched you.

NADIA: I'd never touched you and I thought that you would pull me straight out of my skin.

JOHN: Your dress was a fine fabric, almost as fine as your skin . . . your shoulders . . . I ran my hands across your shoulders. I lifted your hair and put my hand to the nape of your neck.

NADIA: This was the first time . . .

JOHN: Yes.

NADIA: I was facing you. I was cold. We were children.

JOHN: No. A hot summer night. By the ocean.

NADIA: Near enough to smell the sea.

JOHN: We were no longer children.

NADIA: We came inside to dance.

JOHN: We weren't touching. Just dancing close. You were laughing . . . I watched the pulse at the base of your throat . . .

NADIA: I wondered what you would do, how you would do it . . . whether you would promise me things.

JOHN: I talked to you. I was so terrified that I couldn't stop talking . . . all of the things that I told you about . . . from the first time I'd seen you and been afraid to speak.

NADIA: No. You didn't say a word. We were walking, along the beach, not saying anything. And you kissed me. Startled me.

JOHN: I told you I would love you always.

NADIA: We lay down. You put your head on my breast. I pushed you away. Not like that. Not like a child coming to his mother.

JOHN: No. I talked until I had no breath left. I promised you everything I could think of. We were by the road, walking in the roadside. I couldn't stop talking until you kissed me . . . you pushed me by a fence. You put your hands inside my shirt . . . I was afraid to touch you.

NADIA: It was a beach.

JOHN: Another man, another time.

NADIA: No. (*She moves toward him.*) You pulled me out of my skin. When I stood up I was a new person.

JOHN: (*Backing off.*) But I've never touched you.

NADIA: And I don't know your name.

(*A beat.*)

JOHN: Right.

(*A beat.*)

NADIA: It's just as well.

JOHN: Yes. Just as well.

(JOHN *exits.*)

END

JACK HEIFNER's first play, *Casserole*, was produced in 1975 by Playwrights Horizons. "Playwrights" was also one of the original producers of Mr. Heifner's second play, *Vanities*, in 1976. *Patio/Porch* was produced in 1978 at Broadway's Century Theatre. That same year *Music-Hall Sidelights* premiered at the Lion Theatre Company. He followed this in 1980 when *Star Treatment* was produced by the Lion. His other works include *America Was, Tornado, Tropical Depression, Twister,* and the book for the new musical *Smile.* A recipient of a 1977 Creative Artists Public Service grant and a National Endowment for the Arts Fellowship in 1978, Mr. Heifner has a B.F.A. degree from Southern Methodist University. He was elected to New Dramatists in 1981.

BRILLIANTS

Jack Heifner

Setting

The Lobby of the Algonquin Hotel on West 44th Street in
New York City.

Characters

LEE FRANCIS—A writer in his middle thirties. He is dressed
    in a conservative suit and is not a theatrical type.
JAMIE PETTY—A director in his middle thirties. He is very
    similiar to Lee.
INTERVIEWER—A woman in her twenties or thirties.
    Very pushy.

INTERVIEWER: Lee Francis and Jamie Petty are the brilliant
playwright and direct. ˉ of the longest-running show in the
history of the American theatre. I met them recently for
drinks and talk at the famed Algonquin Hotel.

LEE: A Bloody Mary.

JAMIE: I'll have a Bloody Mary.

INTERVIEWER: So what's happening, fellas? What are you
two working on?

JAMIE: He's working on his den.

LEE: I've been moving the furniture about trying to find the
position that will make me start writing again.

INTERVIEWER: That's not exactly what I meant, but . . . tell
me, I've heard that you guys are very old friends.

JAMIE: That's right.

LEE: That's right.

INTERVIEWER: And where did you first meet?

LEE: On our college campus. We were both in the Art Department and we ended up pledging the same fraternity.

JAMIE: Then I dropped out of the fraternity.

LEE: And I dropped out of the fraternity.

JAMIE: And I dropped out of the Art Department.

LEE: Then I dropped out of the Art Department.

JAMIE: And we both ended up in the Theatre Department.

LEE: At the time we were doing things simultaneously.

INTERVIEWER: And that's where you did your first play together?

JAMIE: Yes, indeed. Lee wrote this eccentric musical called *Sqush the Mush* and all the characters were mushrooms. If you were naughty you got punished. You were thrown into a beef stroganoff. It was horrifying.

LEE: Talk about horrifying. Every night, before the show, Jamie locked the entire cast in the men's room. For preparation he made them wail and scream and carry on for a hour . . . in character, of course.

JAMIE: I, at the time being heavily into Gestalt, also locked the theatre. The audience literally got up and stood against the doors waiting for the intermission. We thought that was the neatest thing in the world.

LEE: We upset so many people.

JAMIE: It's a pity we can't alienate audiences now.

INTERVIEWER: And what are you doing now? In the last ten years, since your show has been running, you haven't done another one. Why is that?

JAMIE: Well, I had to take a little time off. I started painting again . . . first time since college. I rented an estate in Connecticut and I began by painting the autumn colors. The leaves. Exteriors. Then it got colder and I had to come inside . . . so I started a series of paintings of the chairs which were in the house. Then the wallpapers. And finally one day I was painting and I looked at the canvas and focused for the first time in about eight years . . . and I realized I was painting the pattern of the carpet. And I said to myself, if I continue staying here and continue painting, I will soon be painting the bristles of the brush. Soon I will be painting the paint. I've got to get out of here! I've got to get back to the theatre.

INTERVIEWER: I see? So, Lee . . . what have you accomplished in the last decade? Have you been painting, too?

LEE: Actually, I wrote one other play. A fifteen-minute piece. It begins with someone holding a salad bowl and singing, "Now I cut the lettuce and put the lettuce in." They do that . . . then sing, "Now I cut the tomato and put the tomato in." And "Now I put on the dressing." And the final twelve minutes consists of furious tossing. Never produced.

JAMIE: All our great ideas are never done.

LEE: We're both heavily into nonlinear work and someday we hope to make it big in the noncommercial theatre.

JAMIE: Right now, we're both just destroyed that what we've done is so commercial that we can't do real art.

INTERVIEWER: Oh, come on. I'm sure you're not destroyed by the fame and money that comes from having a long-running smash.

LEE: But we can't be silly anymore.

JAMIE: We have definitely stopped being silly.

LEE: I mean, you can't be really silly when you're trying to create a serious new show.

INTERVIEWER: Ah ha! So that's what you've been up to?

JAMIE: Oh, you've caught us! Yes, we're forced to admit we've been trying to work on a monumental, new idea.

LEE: It's going to be like this time *I* give the audience beef stroganoff and then ask *them* to write the recipe.

INTERVIEWER: (*To* JAMIE) And what exactly does that mean?

JAMIE: Oh, I don't know what it means . . . but it's brilliant.

LEE: Exactly, I don't know what it means but it's brilliant.

JAMIE: And I think we've got ourselves another hit.

LEE: Unfortunately. Another Bloody Mary?

JAMIE: I'll have another Bloody Mary.

INTERVIEWER: And that's how my interview went with the playwright and director of Broadway's longest-running show. I don't have a clue what they mean, but I'll have a double Bloody Mary.

END

POLLSTER

Jack Heifner

(A woman in her twenties or thirties enters and begins to speak to the audience. She is well dressed and she carries a shopping bag and a note pad. Note: *Current references in this piece should be updated when it is performed.)*

Excuse me—I'm not part of the show, but you look like a sympathetic group of people . . . not unlike myself . . . you go out to the theatre and are looking for answers . . . so I want to share a few things with you.

You see, recently I did my own private survey. I stood on Lexington Avenue between Alexanders and Bloomingdales, and did you know that only 1% of the Americans I interviewed had ever heard of or knew the meaning of the words *leftist guerilla, nouvelle cuisine,* and *gelato.* And yet, 99% of those surveyed were very well acquainted with or knew the meaning of the *enchilada, high heel,* and *missionary position.* Think about it.

And do you realize that only one out of three Americans under thirty can sing the words to the "Star Spangled Banner"? Yet one out of two Americans of that age know all the words to "Beat It?"*(Insert name of current popular song.)*

And speaking of music, did you notice that when Nancy Reagan was introduced at last summer's Republican National Convention, *(Insert name of latest function.)* the band played "You Do Something To Me?" Are lyrics like "do do that voodoo that you do so well" appropriate for a first lady? And don't you just wonder how much someone has paid Jane Wyman to keep her mouth shut? I mean, it seems like everybody and his brother was willing to say they'd jumped into bed with John Kennedy . . . so why will nobody admit they've slept with Reagan? I mean, he was an actor and as bad as he was there has to be some way he got all those jobs.

Anyway, back to my poll. The most interesting political figures of the twentieth century turned out to be: Betty Ford—who overcome addiction to valium and alcohol and had her face lifted. And Mamie Eisenhower, who didn't. Eleanor Roosevelt—who overcame terminal ugliness. And Lynda Bird Johnson, who didn't. And J. Edgar Hoover—who was able to run the F.B.I. for years and keep secret the fact that he was just another old queen.

A sort of useless but stimulating piece of information I gathered is that one out of three Americans would like to eat the Olympic Gold Medal Men's Gymnastics Team. Think about it.

I can't seem to find any answers to these questions: Why are the Reagan children so weird? Why don't they look like their parents? Who are their parents? Why does Reagan act so dopey? I mean, the theme song for his recent campaign might as well have been "Send In the Clowns." (*Insert*: The Theme of his administration might as well be "Happy Talk.")

But everybody loves him. He won by a landslide. I mean, this is the eighties and we're back living in the fifties. We've got a government that's ordering us to "Get married, have a family and go to church." Suddenly the government sounds like my mother.

Well, Mom and America . . . I've tried. I wanted to get married, but no one asked me. I wanted to have kids. I really wanted to believe in God. I'm sorry . . . but I just can't.

So what's going to happen to people like us? My conclusion . . . my survey points this out and the election proves it . . . is that there are more of them out there than we thought. Conservatives, Republicans, Falwells . . . people who are going to force us to pray at school and before meals whether we like it or not. So be careful. They're out to get you. To save your soul.

Unless . . . just unless . . . I'm looking at you and I know you seem to be sympathetic . . . but maybe . . . just maybe . . . you're already one of "them." I mean, you all look too blissed-out. Too clean!

Oh, my God. Excuse me, I seem to have wandered into the wrong place. I'm not part of the show going on here or anywhere for that matter. Excuse me.

(She exits)

SHERRY KRAMER holds MFAs in both Playwriting and Fiction from the Iowa Writers Workshops, and received her undergraduate degree from Wellesley College. She is the recipient of a National Endowment for the Arts Fellowship, and worked for Columbia Pictures as a member of their Writers Workshop. *About Spontaneous Combustion* and *The Release Of a Live Performance* were produced at Brass Tacks Theatre, Minneapolis, in 1982. She was a writer-in-residence at the Bay Area Playwrights Festival in 1982. Ms. Kramer was admitted to New Dramatists in 1981 as the first National member.

HOLD FOR THREE

Sherry Kramer

Cast

SCOTTIE—A woman
BARTEY—A woman
ED—A man

(*They are at the beach, at the water's edge. The horizon exists on a line parallel with the top of the audience.*)

SCOTTIE: (*Excited*) There—(*She points at the horizon, where the moon as just started up.*)

(ED *takes in a huge breath of air.*)

SCOTTIE: She's up—she's up—

BARTEY: This is ridiculous—he's not going to be able to hold his breath while the moon comes up—

SCOTTIE: Come on, come on, look at your watch——

BARTEY: Okay, okay. It is exactly (*Looks at her watch, tells what time it is.*) (_____) and 17 seconds.

SCOTTIE: Let's subtract five seconds to adjust for operator error, shall we?

BARTEY: What do I care, Scottie? Really . . .

SCOTTIE: Okay, now, Ed, the first 30 seconds or so are easy. Just relax and save yourself.

BARTEY: (*Looking at* ED, *shaking her head.*) You're weird.

SCOTTIE: Adjusted time from start?

BARTEY: Uh—23 seconds.

SCOTTIE: Okay. Allllllright. (*Coaching sequences are down directly to* ED, *as excited as possible.*) Now. I want you imagine that

you are in a Movie of the Week disaster film with Evette
Minaux. You are underwater in—in a nuclear submarine.
Evette is trapped in the compartment where Polaris missiles
are armed and ready to fly. You got to hold your breath long
enough to get in, rescue her, disarm six missiles, and save
the world from nuclear holocaust. Got that?

(ED *nods, and mimes spinning open bulkheads, disarming missiles.*)

SCOTTIE: That ought to take him a while. Time?

BARTEY: He's never going to make it—

SCOTTIE: Give me a break. It's almost a third of the way up.

BARTEY: A third—a third? His eyebrows just popped up—

SCOTTIE: The man in the moon does not have—

BARTEY: Well, if he did, that's what we'd—ooooh—here
come the eyes—

SCOTTIE: Time, damn it, time—I got a man here trying to
do a job—

BARTEY: 53 seconds.

SCOTTIE: Okay. Here we go. You're Anne Frank. Three
storm troopers with boots polished to a shine hard enough to
bounce laser beams enter the room. You're hiding in a pile
of dirty laundry. One breath out of you—you'll feel the cold
steel of their bayonets.

(ED *crouches on the floor, his hands covering his head, etc.*)

SCOTTIE: Not bad, huh?

(ED *makes a mezzo, mezzo gesture with one hand.*)

BARTEY: (*Looking closely at* ED.) He's turning blue.

SCOTTIE: (*Looks carefully, too.*) He just didn't shave this
morning, that's all.

BARTEY: And he's shaking, I think—

SCOTTIE: (*Looking at the moon.*) It's close to halfway, wouldn't
you say?

BARTEY: Why is he shaking like that—

SCOTTIE: Oh, differences in temperature in the atmospheric layers, something like that I guess. Distorts the air waves.

BARTEY: No, not the moon. Ed.

SCOTTIE: So he's shaking a little. Look—the bridge is up!

BARTEY: What?

SCOTTIE: Of his nose. Bridge is up, get it?

BARTEY: I hope he doesn't pass out or anything—I mean, what if he hyperventilates in reverse or something—what if he forgets how to breathe—

SCOTTIE: (*As Carl Sagan*) It took the genetic ancestors of Ed Carmichael billions and billions of years to learn to use their lungs—(*As herself*) Even Ed can't screw all that up in three minutes. Time—

BARTEY: One minute, 38 seconds.

SCOTTIE: And the boy is sweating bullets. I know you're gonna love this one, Ed. It's 1969. You're president of your university's SDS. The anti-war protest seems to be coming along fine when—TEAR GAS!!! The pigs have just lobbed in the tear gas—one whiff and you're reduced to a slobbering flower child—you've got to hold your breath long enough to take over the dean's office—GO FOR IT!!!!!

(ED *mimes running, chocking on tear gas, avoiding policemen, etc.*)

SCOTTIE: Time?

BARTEY: One minute, 58.

SCOTTIE: (*Looking at the moon.*) Looks like we're getting into the mouth now. Ed—Ed, hang on, just a couple of lips to go.

(ED *indicates that he just can't go on.*)

Ed—Ed—don't give up now—come on, come on, you can do it—all you have to do is pretend you're—pretend you're —GOD!!! Yes, you're God, and it's Day One of Creation. You've got a whole world of things to make before you get around to breathing the breath of life into Adam, so you hold it—you hold your breath for five days of creatures and firmament and shrubs—only you can do it, Ed, because you're GOD!!

(ED *is past making a rude response to this one. He struggles on.* SCOTTIE *is near hysteria.*)

SCOTTIE: TIME!!!!

BARTEY: Two minutes, 23.

SCOTTIE: THE HOME STRETCH—we're getting into the chin, now. You'll never *guess* what I've saved for the home stretch.

(ED *stops occupying the dean's office and stands, ready.*)

SCOTTIE: You've been unjustly convicted of murder, and sentenced to the gas chamber. You're strapped in—when NEW EVIDENCE PROMPTS A PARDON FROM THE GOVERNOR—but—THE GAS PELLETS HAVE ALREADY BEEN RELEASED!!!!! The guards are rushing to the door to save you—if only you can hold your breath till—

(ED *pretends sitting in the chair, ripping off the restraining straps, going wild trying to hold his breath in the gas chamber.*)

SCOTTIE: TIME!!!!!

BARTEY: Two minutes, 44——

SCOTTIE: They're rushing to save you—

BARTEY: Clearing the chin now—(BARTEY *is now caught up in the excitement.*)

SCOTTIE: They're almost to the door now——

BARTEY: Just this much more to go——(*Makes an eighth of an inch with thumb and first finger, after measuring on the horizon.*)

SCOTTIE: They're at the door——

BARTEY: Two minutes and—you can do it—come on——

SCOTTIE: They're opening the door——

BARTEY: TEN——

SCOTTIE: No, it's stuck——

BARTEY: NINE——

SCOTTIE: They're using brute force——

BARTEY: EIGHT——

SCOTTIE: The guards have asked for help from——

BARTEY: SEVEN——

SCOTTIE: The people from the press——

BARTEY: SIX——

SCOTTIE: The reporters are throwing their weight around——

BARTEY: FIVE——

SCOTTIE: The door starts to give——

BARTEY: FOUR——

SCOTTIE: It starts to give——

BARTEY: THREE——

SCOTTIE: (*Looking at the moon rather than* ED *now.*) Come on, come on, it's starting to give now——

BARTEY: TWO——

SCOTTIE: It's—it's—it's UP!!!!!

(ED *collapses on the floor.*)

BARTEY: ONE—HE DID IT!!!!! THREE MINUTES FLAT!!!!!

(BARTEY *and* SCOTTIE *gaze at the moon for several seconds.*)

SCOTTIE: Beautiful, isn't it, Ed.

ED: (*Raises his head, looks at the moon for the first time.*) Yeah.

(*Beat.*)

BLACKOUT

ROMULUS LINNEY is the author of three novels and many plays, produced in regional theatres throughout the United States, Great Britain, Germany, and Austria. In New York, *The Love Suicide At Schofield Barracks* was presented at the ANTA, *The Sorrows Of Frederick* at St. Clement's, *Holy Ghosts* at Cubiculo, *Old Man Joseph And His Family* by the Chelsea, *The Captivity Of Pixie Shedman* at the Phoenix, *Childe Byron* at Circle Rep, *Goodbye, Howard, El Hermano,* and *Tennessee,* which won an Obie in 1980, at EST, and *Laughing Stock* at the Manhattan Punch Line. He has received both NEA and Guggenheim Fellowships, the Mishima Prize for fiction, and a 1984 award from the American Academy and Institute of Arts and Letters. He has taught fiction and playwriting at many schools, this year at the University of Pennsylvania and at Princeton. As a director, Mr. Linney holds a degree from Yale in '58 and last season directed his own plays for The Philadelphia Festival for New Plays, The Actors Studio, and The Alley Theatre in Houston. He became a New Dramatist in 1978.

MARTHA MILLER

Romulus Linney

(Enter forty-five year old man with drink.)

MAN: Home bed fever 105 crashing down 103 climbing 105 crashing 103 etc. waiting hospital bed phone rings say "Hello?" voice says "Rommy?" (childhood nickname) say "Yep" voice says "Rommy, this is E.C. Green." lucid 105 degree fever plumblines me forty years Peanut Days that canny E.C. Green little kid always smarter than the rest of us always in these better positions all the time acted Rumplestilskin the the seventh grade play me the dumb King all that so I say, "Why, hello E.C. How are you?" he says, "Rommy, you really remember me?" I say all lucid-fever-casual-wise, "Why of course, E.C. How you been?" and we chat me burning up (18 days Lenox Hill Hospital it turned out later) E.C. sent from Madison Tennessee where we grew up to NYC IBM-Hilton-Hotel-Machine-School-Weekend E.C. still living that little town wife five children but still in his good positions and the sort of man who likes to keep some track so we go through some of the names we were, sort of thing, like, "Harold Barns? Rommy, he's working right now at that crooked filling station where Lovely's Drugstore was no I don't remember any Hall girls what? oh Army children oh I see yes oh Sue Neatherly yes she's fine what? who? Martha Miller? Rommy, I didn't know you knew her." There is a silence other end of line. I say, "Oh, yes she moved down from New York City Hell's Kitchen she came from the year before my father died how is she, E.C.?" and he says, "Well, Rommy, funny you asking I went with her a lot later on in high school we were sweethearts I can tell you she meant a lot to me," and scorching fever-vision black tar melting on the Gallatin Pike through the fire strolling cool crisp pert New York City Yankeechild Hell's Kitchen Girl smiling interested in me and I say, "You know E.C. she meant something to me too

Martha Miller very first girl I fell for smash slayed me she did but I was such a dumb little oh God Tennessee hick I couldn't act decently just say something ugly to her all I could do but I never forgot and E.C. now I think about it you know she really was a very remarkable little open person (in the sixth grade for God's sake) I recall her more than once trying to find out what I was really like I think I spit at her for that" and fever-flash first invitation to love flash Martha Miller flash so I say to E.C. again, "E.C. how is she?" and E.C. slowly, "Well, Rommy, Martha Miller is dead she died about two years ago age forty she had married had two children isn't that a shame I can tell you I took it hard" and I say, "Gee, E.C." and hazy hot fever curtains dissolve on the day I went back to school my father buried in the cold cold ground far away from me and Martha Miller walked straight up to me and said she was so sorry my father died but while we'd been away the grass on our front yard hadn't been cut and she wanted me to see about that right away or it would go wild get overgrown and tangled up more than it already was and I told E.C. that and he said, "Yes, that sounds like her she was always a sensible girl practical and encouraging," so we went right on through Murray Siddens and Mary Jean Cole and all the rest of them and then said goodbye and two hours later I was in Lenox Hill left lobar pneumonia doctors nurses wife daughter friends but in my fever dreams that little girl on the day my soul bereft of its father faced a world of death and losses, there she was, pert smiling interested Martha Miller plus of course whatever her married name well whatever married name Martha Miller in my turn I am sorry you're dead and I can't send you my books ask you to plays for a drink in Hell's Kitchen give you something back for your gifts of love and courage so: I will just get well as you would want me to and I will mow my lawn and not let the weeds grow wild but salute now for once at least the beautiful beautiful child who invited me to live instructing me it is never the ending that is important but always the beginning.

(*He drinks to her. Exit* MAN.)

SWANS

Romulus Linney

Characters
ABEL—a retired wheat farmer
LUCILLE—his wife

Place
A trailer camp in Florida

Time
The present

(*Two aluminum-plastic beach chairs. Moonlight. Enter* LUCILLE, *with a small tape recorder and a cassette.*)

LUCILLE: Come on out, Father. I want you to hear this.

(*She puts the cassette into the recorder. Enter her husband* ABEL, *opening a can of beer for her, and one for himself.*)

ABEL: Here's your beer, Mother. Let 'er rip.

(LUCILLE *takes the beer, plays the cassette. An orchestra plays "Clair de Lune." They listen.* LUCILLE *sighs.*)

LUCILLE: Classic of the Night, says here. This little piece of it means moonlight. Who'd ever think a body could get so much pleasure out of one little tune?

ABEL: You ought to, you play it enough.

(*It gets darker.*)

Whup, there it goes, Mother. Your moon. Right behind a cloud.

LUCILLE: Oh fish, It was pretty, a-shining on the lake.

ABEL: Hoped we'd get a look at the camp swans in that moonlight.

LUCILLE: Swans in the moonlight. Pleasures of Florida.

ABEL: Yep. Beer, trailer, swans.

LUCILLE: Retirement, Father.

ABEL: Retirement, Mother.

(*Pause. "Clair de Lune" plays.*)

LUCILLE: Father.

ABEL: Yes, Mother?

LUCILLE: You think we did right, coming here?

ABEL: I do.

LUCILLE: We could have farmed another two years, maybe more.

ABEL: But we didn't.

LUCILLE: I know we didn't, and I know I said yes, all right, but now, I don't know.

ABEL: Don't know what, Mother?

LUCILLE: If we should have come here.

(*The piece of "Clair de Lune" ends, fading away, replaced on the cassette by a Strauss waltz.* LUCILLE *turns off the recorder, rewinds the cassette.*)

I just don't know.

ABEL: Yes, you do. Say it.

LUCILLE: Well, I miss my children!

ABEL: (*Quietly*) Do you?

LUCILLE: Well, yes! (*Pause*) But it is peaceful here. I do like that.

ABEL: So do I. No crazy phone calls in the middle of the night. Running around marrying, divorcing. Some other man's wife, some other woman's man. Whiskey, dope, pistols twice and a shotgun once.

LUCILLE: They got in such trouble. Every one of them.

ABEL: Four trips to the courthouse. Half my crop going to a goddamn lawyer every other year. Enough, Mother. They're growed up now. Let 'em untangle their own lives, and leave us to find a little peace in ours!

LUCILLE: But why? That's what I keep wondering about. Why?

ABEL: We don't know why. Children go crazy. Way it is. We done our best by 'em, left 'em half the farm, now to hell with it. We've earned our rest!

LUCILLE: We gave 'em the farm but that was all. What I keep thinking about, Father, is what we didn't give them. Couldn't give them. What we had together. Always had together.

ABEL: Mother, I don't think anybody can give anybody that.

LUCILLE: But why not! I tried to tell Sarah once, what it was like, seeing you the first time, and not liking you at all, and then you just waiting for me, and waiting for me—

ABEL: Well, I knew, Mother. I just knew.

LUCILLE: And from the first, everything, I mean first TIME together, too, well, well, now—

ABEL: Mother, stop fretting about this.

LUCILLE: But it was good! It was always good! God help us, Father, it is now!

ABEL: Yes, it is.

LUCILLE: Then why not for them! Not one of them! What is it we have, just took for granted, they can't never find at all?

ABEL: Now, Mother, hush—

LUCILLE: I never in my life wanted no man but you! And if what you always tell me's the truth—

ABEL: Truth, Mother. Only time I tried anybody else, I got sick you know that.

LUCILLE: Then why? Why? What did we have all them years, working and sweating and farming and making do, they couldn't have too? What did we do wrong?

ABEL: Nothing! They did all that! Just hush!

LUCILLE: What did God give us, that He kept from them?

(*It gets brighter.*)

ABEL: Look, Mother. There's your moonlight again. Play that thing, if you want to, and settle down.

LUCILLE: All right. (*She plays "Clair de Lune" again. Pause.*)

ABEL: There, by God! Look!

(*They both point, staring at the lake.*)

LUCILLE: Swans, Father.

ABEL: Swans. Strange looking critters. Ain't they. Mother?

LUCILLE: I don't think I like them so much.

ABEL: Because they're mean. Look good, but they're cold and mean inside. All took up with theirselves. Come between two swans, you get pecked to death.

LUCILLE: Who'd want to come between 'em?

ABEL: I don't know. Somebody.

(*Pause. Music.*)

LUCILLE: "The Swan is a beauty and not a fake,
          Two are better, upon the lake."

ABEL: Where'd you hear that?

LUCILLE: Read it, yesterday.

ABEL: Where?

LUCILLE: *Reader's Digest.*

ABEL: Oh.

LUCILLE: It was in some article about zoos.

(*The moonlight fades as the music ends.*)

PETER MALONEY has worked extensively in theatre, film, and television as a writer, director, and actor. His plays include *American Garage*, which was presented as a full-length at the Aspen Playwrights Conference and in its original one-act form, *Last Chance Texaco*, as part of Ensemble Studio Theatre's "Marathon '81." Ensemble Studio also produced his plays *Bicycle Boys, Lost and Found*, and *Pastoral, or Recollections of Country Life*. Samuel French published *Lost and Found* soon after its first production, and will publish *Pastoral* and *Last Chance Texaco* this fall. Mr. Maloney wrote the foreword to John Byrne's *The Slab Boys*, published recently in Glasgow, after directing the American and New York premieres of that play. For several years he was a regular contributor of articles on theatre and the arts to the magazine *Changes*. He is a life member of the Actors Studio and became a New Dramatist in 1983.

BETWEEN THE ACTS

Peter Maloney

Characters

MR. LYNCH   Late middle to old age
MRS. LYNCH   The same
THEATREGOERS   Various ages.

Place
The lobby of a theatre

Time
Between the acts of a play

(*Lights up on the lobby of a theatre, between the acts of a play. On one wall of the lobby is a poster advertising a series of plays, as in summer stock. The intermission crowd assembles. As they buy their drinks or coffee and light up cigarettes,* MR. *and* MRS. LYNCH *enter the lobby from the theatre.* MRS. LYNCH *is perusing her program as* MR. LYNCH *looks around.* MR. LYNCH *is somewhat deaf. After a moment.*)

MR. LYNCH: Wish I still smoked.

MRS. LYNCH: Well, you don't.

MR. LYNCH: What?

MRS. LYNCH: (*Louder*) *You don't smoke.*

MR. LYNCH: I know that. You made me quit.

MRS. LYNCH: (*Fishing in her bag.*) The *doctors* made you quit.

MR. LYNCH: I'd love a cigarette.

MRS. LYNCH: (*Taking a cigarette and lighter from purse.*) Well you can't have one.

(MRS. LYNCH *lights her cigarette as* MR. LYNCH *watches her.*)

MR. LYNCH: How can you do that?

MRS. LYNCH: (*Taking a satisfying drag.*) *I'm* not a diabetic.

MR. LYNCH: Right in front of me.

MRS. LYNCH: How do you like the play so far?

MR. LYNCH: What?

(MRS. LYNCH *doesn't answer, just smokes, looking over the lobby crowd.*)

That girl is good.

MRS. LYNCH: The blonde one, yes.

MR. LYNCH: She talks right up.

MRS. LYNCH: She projects.

MR. LYNCH: She what?

MRS. LYNCH: *Projects.* That's what they call it.

MR. LYNCH: You can hear her.

MRS. LYNCH: Projecting.

MR. LYNCH: Almost every word.

(*Pause.*)

She looks familiar.

MRS. LYNCH: She was in the play last week.

MR. LYNCH: That's it. But she was a redhead in that one.

(*Pause*)

What was the play last week?

MRS. LYNCH: I don't remember.

(*Pause*)

MR. LYNCH: I liked it better than this one.

MRS. LYNCH: This is a *drama*. Last week's play was a *melodrama*.

MR. LYNCH: That explains it. What was the name of it?

MRS. LYNCH: The poster's over there. Go look.

(MR. LYNCH *starts toward the poster on the wall.* MRS. LYNCH *watches him go, speaks to someone standing next to her.*)

MRS. LYNCH: My husband just had three toes removed. Last month. From his right foot. You'd never know it, would you, to see him walk. Of course he can't run, and he'd be in trouble if he had to climb a tree in a hurry. Walking used to be his business. He's a retired policeman.

(*She goes back to reading her program as* MR. LYNCH *gets to the poster on the other side of the lobby. He speaks to a person standing next to him.*)

MR. LYNCH: Could you spare a cigarette? . . . Thanks, I'm trying to quit. (*Lights the cigarette.*) What do you think of the play? (*Pause*) You know what I think is wrong with the theatre? It's not real enough. It's not enough like real life. Real life is dramatic. (*Pause*)

Listen, I have an idea for a play. Tell me what you think. The main character is a retired policeman. He's married thirty-two years to a woman he can't stand. So one day he reaches the breaking point. She says the same something in the same way once too often, so what he does, he shoots her, right in the middle of *Another World*. With his police revolver. (*He pats the breast pocket of his coat on the left side.*) They let you keep it after you retire. Now that'd make a good play.

(*The lights blink, signalling the end of intermission.* MR. LYNCH *checks the poster, puts out his cigarette, heads back toward his wife. As he gets to her . . .*)

Dramatic License.

MRS. LYNCH: What?

MR. LYNCH: That was the play last week. *Dramatic License.*

MRS. LYNCH: Oh, yes. She went to Juilliard.

MR. LYNCH: Who did?

MRS. LYNCH: The girl. The blonde.

MR. LYNCH: She's a musician too?

MRS. LYNCH: The acting school. That's where she learned to speak so well.

MR. LYNCH: She talks right up.

MRS. LYNCH: Projects, is what she does.

MR. LYNCH: She does. You can hear her. Almost every word.

(*They go into the theatre as the lights fade.*)

THE END

DENNIS MCINTYRE became a New Dramatist in the fall of 1979. His play *Modigliani* was produced at the Astor Place Theatre and later acquired for film by Keith Barish Productions. His play *Split Second* is being produced at Theatre Four, and it has been optioned for film by Motown Records. He was born in Detroit and educated at the University of Michigan and Carnegie-Mellon University. He has received the Avery and Jule Hopwood Award in Playwriting and Fiction, an MCA Fellowship in Playwriting, two Shubert Fellowships in Playwriting, a Rockefeller Grant for Production, a Tufts University Commission for Playwriting, the "Playbill" Award for Playwriting, and a National Endowment for the Arts in Playwriting. His new play, *National Anthems*, was presented at the 1984 O'Neil Playwrights Conference, and it has been optioned for a New York production. He has just completed a novel, *The Divine Child*, and he will be teaching a playwriting workshop at the University of Michigan in 1985.

THE BOYFRIEND

Dennis McIntyre

(*A bare space. A single spot on* CAMERON. *He sits on a wooden chair. He is neatly groomed and well-dressed. His hands rest on his knees. He never moves them until the end.*)

CAMERON: If you really want to know, my name is Cameron, and, when I met her, I had a swimming scholarship. That's why we went to the same school. We dated for eleven months and three days before it ended.

The night it happened, I was staying downstairs on their couch. She'd already told me that I wouldn't be staying on their couch anymore. We'd be good friends. That's what she said. And she'd always come to watch me swim.

Her father was a surgeon. Her mother liked to entertain. Her father liked to carve, even on the weekends, so I knew all about the knives in the kitchen. My father always left the carving to my mother. He managed an A&P in West Los Angeles, and he didn't know about the finer things in life.

I had to get the carving knife out of the dishwasher. It was stainless steel. It was imported from West Germany. Everything in their house was imported. My parents had a vase from my grandmother—it was supposed to be from Mexico. I rinsed the knife in hot water. It still smelled like roast beef even after I dried it.

I went upstairs. I kept curling my toes into their carpet. I remember thinking about my own house, and all the linoleum on the basement stairs. I didn't bother to get dressed. I was wearing my white Jockey shorts. I have a swimmer's body, and I look much better without my clothes.

I passed her parents' bedroom. I could hear a television set. Very low. They were watching *Johnny Carson*. That's the kind of people they were when they weren't having dinner parties or operating. I opened her door. If she'd locked it, things might have turned out differently. I could hear her breathing. It was relaxed. It was content. It didn't include me.

I moved to the window and began counting the cars going across the Triboro Bridge—trying to get my mind off her breathing—pretending every third car belonged to me.

I got tired of counting the cars. None of them met my expectations. I walked over to her bed. I couldn't see her face. She had long, brown hair, and it'd flopped forward in her sleep. I could see the tip of her nose. It curved upward, like her mother's. I pulled back the blanket, and then I pulled back the sheet. I did it very gently. I didn't want to wake her up, and I didn't. I wanted it to be a surprise. She was wearing a man's white pajama top and white panties. The man's pajama top didn't belong to me, and I couldn't imagine her going out and buying it for herself. If I hadn't seen her in that man's white pajama top, then things might have been different.

I remember thinking, just before I ended it, "Let's see what your fucking father can do about this one."

She didn't cry out. I expected something. My name maybe. But she didn't say a thing. When I rolled her over, her mouth and eyes were open. She was staring straight up at me, but she was pretending not to recognize me. It was just like her.

I went back to the window. I decided to ignore the blood and count every fourth car. I kept counting and counting. The twenty-fifth time I counted, I ended up with a white Mercedes-Benz, and I knew everything would be all right.

(*He smiles—a frozen smile. He runs his right hand through his hair, and then holds the back of his neck.*)

I loved listening to her speak French, even though I couldn't understand a word of it. I think that's why she did it around me. But I forgave her. And I always will.

(*He remains frozen. The spot slowly fades out.*)

THE END

ERIC OVERMYER is currently Literary Manager of Playwrights Horizons and an Artistic Associate of Center Stage, Baltimore. His plays have been performed in New York, Seattle, Los Angeles, Baltimore, and Denver. *Native Speech* received its premiere in 1983 at Los Angeles Actors Theatre and subsequently was produced at Stage One in Dallas and Center Stage, and was published in *Wordplays 3* and in an acting edition by Broadway Play Publishing. His *On the Verge* has been done in workshop at the Denver Center Theatre and at Center Stage and will be produced at Center Stage during the 1984–85 season. He became a New Dramatist in 1984.

HAWKER

Eric Overmyer
A Four-minute Hector for One Woman

For Brenda Wehle

Cast

LUCILLE, a Hawker of Marvelous Inventions

(LUCILLE *appears before the audience, dressed extravagantly.*)

LUCILLE: (*Formally*) Lucille? Is that you? (*Beat*) I just love pop music allusions, don't you? What have we here? (*She unpacks her wares. A glass.*)

LUCILLE: Oh, this is lovely. Cheese drink. It's to die. Sip? Cheddar shake. A little on the viscous side, I admit. Brie too is an acquired taste. Whenever I'm in a room with a ripe brie I am reminded of an old boyfriend. But that is another story.

(*She displays a medallion.*)

LUCILLE: Thinking about Genghis puts me in mind of this. I know you're all going to want one. Yes, it's what you've all been waiting for, you've heard about it at the health club juice bar, wiping the carrot froth off your upper lip, you've read the subway ads in Spanish, you've wished for one at Area in the wee wee hours. Say no more. A detector of sexually transmitted diseases. Great. Am I right or what? Who needs the guess work? Life's too short. Changes colors just like those mood rings I sold you last time I was here. Take it into Carumba's, it's Fourth of July fireworks. You have not seen colors like this since mescaline. I don't care what they say now, the sixties were not half bad. Let's see, what else?

(*She displays a business card.*)

LUCILLE: This is more in the line of a service rather than a good. It's an agent for your life. Somebody to negotiate for you at the cleaners, stand in line at the bureau of motor vehicles, the post office, the bank, Balducci's. Somebody to duke it out with your ex-, your present significant other, your boss, even with Mom.

Why do you have to be a rich and famous asshole to have your own personal major-domo? Is ten percent too much to pay for a stress-free environment? I think not!

(*She puts card away.*)

LUCILLE: (*High dudgeon*) "Las cucarachas entran—
                          Pero no pueden salir!"

(*Beat*)

I wish I knew the one for hemmorhoids. The last thing I need is hemmorhoids. Sounds so much better in Spanish, somehow.

(*She puts on cardboard 3D glasses.*)

LUCILLE: Nice, huh? At last they've found a use for those millions of glasses. These are for watching German art. They make it funny. The give it all those things German art inevitably lacks. Irony, a light touch, a spirit of fun—in short, a sense of humor. No longer is the phrase "German sense of humor" a horrible oxymoron thanks to these nifty little glasses. A must for Pina Bausch concerts or Kroetz plays. Just an aside—can you imagine having sex with either Pina Bausch or Franz Xavier Kroetz? They're at the top of my list to look out for.

(*She straps on a red clown nose.*)

LUCILLE: I know what you're thinking. Lucille—is that you? Oh, Lucille, come on. Please. A clown nose? We can get a clown nose at our favorite novelty emporium. What do we need with a clown nose? We depend on you, Lucille, for the scarce and unusual, the frightening and the purgative, the exquisitely absurd, the faintly ridiculous. Speaking of the exquisitely absurd, what are we all going to do now that Ronco has gone out of business? Vegamatic? The little gadget that scrambled the egg in the shell? Operators are standing by!

Not available in any store! It really really works! (*Sighs*) An institution has passed. The end of an era. I hope all of you out there are holding on to your Vegamatics because they are WORTH SOMETHING NOW! Big buckage. Major league clammage. Boo-coo dinero.

(*Shakes herself.*)

Lucille, you sentimental old Bozo. You haven't even told the folks about the nose. And time is running out.

(*She puts on a hat to go with her nose.*)

LUCILLE: Feeling blue? Is "anomie" your middle name? Out of step and alienated? Hate the theatre? Wonder what planet the critics are from? Can't get it up to find *People* magazine a laff riot like you used to? Only mildly amused by *Enquirer* headlines like "Bo Derek—Herpes Scare!"? Find you're not surprised by the *Times* article that 50% of America does not believe in evolution? Feel trapped in New York, because bad as it is, you know at least three people who laugh at the same appalling shit you do? Wonder why no one seems to notice that our acting president isn't playing with a full deck? I know what ails you, Bunky. I know about that free-floating anxiety, that subtle sunset depression. I know it's not your relationship with your mother that's got you down—it's the state of the union.

(*Taps her nose.*)

You may think this is a clown nose—but it's not. It is an Irony Relaxer. And that seems to me to be a necessity for modern life. Wear it to the theatre, wear it to the laundromat, wear it while reading the *Times*, or better yet, the *Post*, wear it while watching TV news, wear it watching the Ron and Nancy Show, wear it watching Mary Lou Retton, wear it whenever you just cannot fucking believe it. You'll feel better. It really really works. Not available in any store. Operators are standing by.

(*Beat*)

Yes, I know one must have a sense of irony to survive. But sometimes you just got to give it a rest.

(*She collects her stuff.*)

LUCILLE: My four minutes are up. Gotta run.

MAC WELLMAN's first plays were commissioned and produced by K.R.O. Radio in The Netherlands. One of these, *Fama Combinatoria*, was subsequently staged at the Theatre "De Brakke Grond" in Amsterdam in 1975, and later performed in ten other Dutch cities and Belgium. In 1976 his play *The Memory Theatre of Giordano Bruno* was produced at the W.P.A. in Washington, D.C. A K.R.O. version of the piece, completed in 1979, was selected to represent The Netherlands at the *Prix d'Italia* competition for radio-drama. In the same year his play *Starluster* was staged at the American Place Theatre, and later published in the Performing Arts Journal's *Wordplays* anthology. In 1982 his one-act *The Self-Begotten* appeared at the Ensemble Studio Theatre's Marathon. As Playwright-in-Residence at the Bay Area Playwrights Festival in 1983 he worked on the *Phantomnation* collaboration. Recent productions include *The Professional Frenchman* at the Brass Tacks Theatre in Minneapolis and *Energumen* at Soho Rep in New York. As Playwright-in-Residence at NYU he adapted Lope de Vega's *Dog in the Manger*. He edited *Breathing Space*, a collection of sound-text art for *Black Box*, a literary magazine on cassette tape. Wellman also has edited an anthology of new American drama entitled *Theatre of Wonders*, forthcoming from Sun & Moon Press. His poetry, plays, and articles have appeared in many publications. Wellman's books of poetry include *In Praise of Secrecy* (1977), *Satires* (1984), and the forthcoming *Art of the Apostrophe*. His play *Harm's Way* is published by Broadway Play Publishing.

MICHAEL S. ROTH is a composer whose work with Mac Wellman includes *Starluster*, *The Nain Rouge*, and *Energumen*. His chamber compositions include *No End to Stand On*, *Stretch*, and the opera *Hopi Prophecies*. He lives in New York, has taught at Stanford, and is the resident composer at the LaJolla Playhouse.

NO SMOKING PIECE

Mac Wellman

(Scene: Empty, except for a WOMAN, *seated center in a puddle of light, watching TV and smoking. Her* VOICE, *another woman, is seated in a chair several yards off to one side. The play begins with a pause.)*

VOICE:
I bought a gun.
I bought a gun and learned how to use it.
I bought a gun and hid it under my pillow.

(Pause.)

A long time ago I quit smoking.

(Pause.)

It was still early so I turned on the TV.
The Republican convention. Wheels within wheels.
His hair was green, so I turned off the TV
and sat in the dark, smoking.

(Pause.)

My old boyfriend sold junk jewelry.
He had this junk jewelry shop
in Bangkok. One day one of the
native workers looked green. So
my boyfriend took all his boys to the
doctor. He called them "boys" and
they called him "tuan" (*two on*). So they all
traisped off to the doctor to discover
the meaning of this strange greenness
The "boys" were all healthy, but
my boyfriend had tuberculosis.

(Pause.)

He had to give up drinking.
He had to give up smoking.

(*Pause.*)

Seeing the President like that on TV
with his hair all green, well, it
reminded me of the last time
I was in Amsterdam.
There was this extremely fascinating
exhibition in the Stock Exchange.
It was called "Torture Instruments
through the Ages", and I thought
how appropriate
for an exhibition
of this kind
to be housed
in the Stock Exchange.

(*Pause.*)

It was then I decided to stop smoking.
It was then I decided to come back home and vote.
It was then I decided to break up
with this creep of a boyfriend.

(*Pause.*)

Well, it was getting late so I turned on the TV.
It was the Democratic convention.
I turned it off. I don't like flea circuses.
It was the Republican convention.
I turned it off. Too much green hair.
It was the Olympics.
I went to the ice box
for another beer. I went to sleep.

(*Pause.*)

When I woke up it was about one-thirty
and there was this man on TV and he was
saying: "Don't you think it's about time
for a real change?"

(*Pause.*)

"My name is Gus Hall." he said.

(*Pause.*)

"Vote Communist." he said.

THE PORCUPINE MAN

Mac Wellman

(*Scene: A small room or closet. The ceiling is painted to represent the starry night.* NARRATOR *and* SHAMAN *stand close together in dim light. The latter's mask is placed on the back of the actor's head so that when he changes into the* PORCUPINE MAN *he can simply wheel about to reveal his new aspect. The meteor is an egglike cloak which the* SHAMAN *encloses around himself (except for his toes). The fire in the sky is an overhead light. The* PORCUPINE MAN's *song is recorded on a cassette player which he carries with him. The speakers may either be affixed to the walls of the closet, or concealed on his clothing. NOTE: Michael Roth's setting of the song follows the text of the play.*)

NARRATOR: One night in deepest Siberia, in the Yakutsk region to be precise, one Urosh, son of Caka, grandson of Nogaj, and a shaman of our people, had a vision. *I see*, he said . . .

(SHAMAN *shakes his rattle.*)

I see a great bonfire in the heavens . . .

NARRATOR: At that moment a great fire appeared in the sky . . . (*He turns on the overhead light.*) A great fire appeared and streaked across the heavens.

SHAMAN: It is an omen! A great monster will be born among us!

NARRATOR: Shrieked Urosh, just as a great stone fell out of the sky and crashed to earth, precisely at the point where poor Urosh had been standing. (*Pause.*) Only the pointed tips of his sandals protruded from under the massive stone. All the trees of the Yakutsk region of Siberia lay like matchsticks, radiating in vast circles from the point where Urosh had been struck.

(*Drum roll and fanfare.*)

Soon after, the Porcupine Man appeared among us . . . (*He whirls about.*) covered from head to toe with long, quill-like hairs, except for the tip of his nose and the palms of his hands. (*He holds out his hands.*) At first we were horrified. For the monster carried an enormous axe. After a brief pause, and a meditative scratch, he announced, in a booming voice:

PORCUPINE MAN: My name Omurtag, the happy woodsman.

NARRATOR: And pointing to a large fir, which had not been toppled by the great stone, he sang:

PORCUPINE MAN: I'm gonna climb that tree and cut it down.

(*His song begins here and continues to end.*)

NARRATOR: The Porcupine Man stayed with us. Worked with us. Shared the fruits of our labor with us. He was a hard worker and a pleasant companion. He married. His wife Umar bore him five children. All porcupines like him. (*He shows photographs.*) He became a town elder, a respected man in the Yakutsk region. (*Pins a medal on the* PORCUPINE MAN.) So far as anyone can tell he lived a perfectly normal life, a credit to the community, and to the prophetic powers of Urosh, our late shaman, except that when the forest had grown back . . .

PORCUPINE MAN: I strode back into the forest and disappeared.

(*See score on following pages.*)

I'm Gonna Climb That Tree
and Cut It Down

(FOR S₁, S₂, A or CT, T₁, T₂, B)

music – MICHAEL S. ROTH
words – JOHN WELLMAN

SCHREIER/ROTH *

SCHREIER/ROTH *

SCHREIER/ROTH *

COMPOSED FOR
WELLMAN'S
EPIC DRAMA
THE PORCUPINE
MAN

NYC 12/16/83

(PREMIERED AT THE PEASLEE
CHRISTMAS PARTY THAT NIGHT)

SCHREIER/ROTH *

AUGUST WILSON was born in Pittsburgh, Pennsylvania and now lives in St. Paul, Minnesota. In addition to being a member of New Dramatists, he is an Associate Playwright at the Playwrights Center in Minneapolis where he has been awarded a McKnight Fellowship in Playwriting. His play *Ma Rainey's Black Bottom* was first presented at the Eugene O'Neill Theater Center's National Playwrights Conference in 1982, premiered at Yale Repertory Theatre in April '84, and opened at Broadway's Cort Theatre in October 1984. *Fences,* presented at the 1983 National Playwrights Conference, is scheduled for the Yale Repertory Theatre's 84–85 season. *Joe Turner's Come and Gone* (Formerly *Mill Hand's Lunch Bucket*) was selected for work at the 1984 National Playwrights Conference. Among his other plays are *Jitney, Fullerton Street,* and *The Coldest Day of the Year.* Mr. Wilson has been awarded Fellowships in Playwriting from the Bush and Rockefeller Foundations. He is also a poet and his work has appeared in numerous magazines and periodicals and Harper and Row's anthology, *Black Poets of the 20th Century.* He became a New Dramatist in 1983.

THE JANITOR

August Wilson

Characters
SAM
MR. COLLINS

Setting
A Hotel Ballroom

(SAM *enters pushing a broom near the lectern. He stops and reads the sign hanging across the ballroom.*)

SAM: National . . . Conference . . . on . . . Youth.

(*He nods his approval and continues sweeping. He gets an idea, stops, and approaches the lectern. He clears his throat and begins to speak. His speech is delivered with the literacy of a janitor. He chooses his ideas carefully. He is a man who has approached life honestly, with both eyes open.*)

SAM: I want to thank you all for inviting me here to speak about youth. See . . . I's fifty-six years old and I knows something about youth. The first thing I knows . . . is that youth is sweet before flight . . . its odor is rife with specula tion and its resilience . . . that's its bounce back . . . is re-markable. But it's that sweetness that we victims of. All of us. Its sweetness . . . and its flight. One of them fellows in that Shakespeare stuff said, "I am not what I am." See. He wasn't like Popeye. This fellow had a different understand-ing. 'I am not what I am.'' Well, neither are you. You are just what you have been . . . whatever you are now. But what you are now ain't what you gonna become . . . even though it is with you now . . it's inside you now this instant. Time . . . see, this how you get to this . . . Time ain't changed. Its just moved. Or maybe it ain't moved . . . maybe it just changed. It don't matter. We are all victims of the sweetness of youth and the time of its flight. See . . . just like you I forgot who I am. I forgot what happened first. But I know the river I step into now . . . is not the same river I stepped into twenty years ago. See. I know that much. But I have forgotten the name of the river . . . I have forgotten the names of the gods . . . and like everybody else I have tried to fool them with my dancing . . . and guess at their faces. It's the same with everybody. We don't have to mention no names. Ain't nobody innocent. We are all victims of ourselves. We have all had our hand in the soup . . . and made the music play just so. See, now . . . this what I call wrestling with Jacob's angel. You lay down at night and that angel come to wrestle with you. When you wrestling with that angel you bargaining for you future. See. And what you need to bargain with is that sweetness of youth. So . . . to the youth of the United States I says . . . don't spend that sweetness too fast! 'Cause you gonna need it. See. I's fifty-six years old and I done found that out. But it's all the same. It all comes back on you . . . just like reaping and sowing. Down and out ain't nothing but being caught up in the balance of what you put down. If you down and out and things ain't going right for you . . . you can bet you done put a down payment on your troubles. Now you got to pay up on the balance. That's as true as I'm standing here. Sometimes you can't see it like that. The last note on Gabriel's horn always gets lost when you get to realizing you done heard the first. See, it's just like. . . .

MR. COLLINS: (*Entering*) Come on, Sam . . . let's quit wasting time and get this floor swept. There's going to be a big important meeting here this afternoon.

SAM: Yessuh, Mr. Collins. Yessuh.

(SAM *goes back to sweeping as the lights go down to——*)

BLACK

DICK D. ZIGUN grew up in P.T. Barnum's hometown, Bridgeport, CT, and has wanted to be an American showman ever since. He is Founder and Artistic Director of Coney Island, USA, Inc.—a non-profit Museum/Theatre for the creative preservation of American popular culture, and produces the annual *Mermaid Parade* (*Theater* Magazine cover story, Winter 1983); *Sideshows by the Seashore* and other exotic events such as *Tricks & Treats at the Wax Musee* (*The Drama Review*, Spring 1982). He is a graduate of Bennington College and The Yale School of Drama and has written articles on such subjects as amusement parks, April Fools Day, burlesque, and street performers for the *Daily News* and other publications. His play, *Three Unnatural Acts*, has surfaced at the Mark Taper Forum in L.A.; Eureka Theatre in S.F.; Portland Art Museum in Oregon; and Franklin Furnace in N.Y. *Lover's Leap* received its world premiere at The People's Light and Theatre Company in Summer 1984 and his melodrama, *His Master's Voice*, will be seen in New York early in 1985. Mr. Zigun became a New Dramatist in 1981 and went swimming with the Polar Bear Club on New Year's Day 1984.

THE THREE-MINUTE MANIFESTO FOR AN UNCLE SAM ON STILTS
Dick D. Zigun

(Music by Chuck Berry)

UNCLE SAM: (*Enters on stilts wearing traditional costume.*)

Vote for me.
Vote for me.
Vote for me and everybody's gonna find a boyfriend or
    girlfriend.
Vote for me and I said everybody find a boyfriend or
    girlfriend.
Vote for me and join the party.

(*Several Americans enter.*)
(*Play* BACK IN THE USA *by Chuck Berry. They dance.*)

Vote for me and spend more time at the beach.
Vote for me and your city will learn how to party like
    New Orleans during Mardi Gras week.
Vote for me and find out the truth about UFOs and
    about Lee Harvey Oswald.
Vote for me and Lucky Strikes no longer cause cancer.
Vote for me and place bets on your favorite tattoo
    parlor, pool parlor, or beauty parlor being picked
    the daily instant national landmark.
Vote for me and every pizza parlor gets coal ovens and
    a Wurlitzer jukebox, two plays for two bits.
Vote for me and bring back tomatoes.
Vote for me and get fireworks every Tuesday night at
    eleven.
Vote for me and we can put a new paint job on a late
    40's pick-up truck, gas it up, rob a bank, and put

a cool million dollars in the glove compartment and
drive to Coney Island and see Slim of Slim's
Shootin' Gallery, the last live ammo shootin'
gallery left in the east. Now Slim owns some 300
guns and I can get us a spare parts rifle for
sixty bucks with no registration and no way to be
traced . . . you may not want to do this at
all . . . but
Vote for me because I have good connections.
Vote for me and the *National Enquirer* becomes a full-
color glossy.
Vote for me and it's okay to joyride again . . . as long
as you buckle your seatbelt.
Vote for me and make them stop screwin' with the
weather.
Vote for me and always have hot water.
Vote for me if you want guarantees Alaska stays the
coolest state in the union.
Vote for me and Nevada will once more be known as a
state of mind by virtue of vice rather than
geography.
Vote for me and New York becomes the capital of the
world while Los Angeles remains the capital of
America.

(*Pause.* BACK IN THE USA *fades.*)

Vote for me and we'll change the National Anthem
every once and a while.

(*The Americans join hands, sway back and forth and softly hum the
Chuck Berry song.*)

Vote for me and "Life, Liberty, and The Pursuit of Hap-
piness" becomes the new Pledge of Allegiance.
Vote for me and anything you want they got it right
here in the USA.
Vote for me and anything you want they got it right
here in the USA.

Vote for me and anything you want they got it right
here in the USA.
Vote for me.
Vote for me.
Vote for me.

UNTIMELY DEATH WITH DOGS IN DETAIL
The Murder Mystery That Asks
the Question: Who Died?

Dick D. Zigun

ACT ONE/Scene One

(*Very dim light.*)

STAGE MANAGER: Act One. Scene One. Friday the 13th. The Condo:

(*Sound Cues: Breaking glass. Cat. Gun shot.*)

AN ACTOR: Drip — Drip — Drip — Drip . . . (*Continues*)

ANOTHER ACTOR: Ring — Ring —— Ring — Ring

ANOTHER ACTOR: Knock — Knock

SECOND ACTOR: Ring — Ring —— Ring — Ring

FIRST ACTOR: Drip — Drip — Drip — Drip . . . (*Fade out*)

ACT ONE/Scene Two

STAGE MANAGER: Scene Two. Thirteen days later. Scharfstein's Funeral Parlor:

CRYING ACTOR: The thirteen-month husband.

ANOTHER CRYING ACTOR: The wealthy ex-husband.

ANOTHER CRYING ACTOR: The better-looking exhusband.

ANOTHER CRYING ACTOR: The hair stylist with the cocaine habit.

ANOTHER CRYING ACTOR: The bouncer at the latest afterhours club.

MANY CRYING ACTRESSES: The past and current Mah Jongg players among her aunt's best friends who remember her since she was so high.

(BLACKOUT)

ACT ONE/Scene Three

STAGE MANAGER: Scene Three. Later that evening. 13th Street:

CRIMINAL: Bang! Bang! Bang! Bang!

COP: Bang! Bang! Click!

CRIMINAL: Bang! Bang! Click! Click! Pow! Socko!

COP: Pow! Pow! Kick! Thud! Krunch! Pow! Crash!

CRIMINAL: Buckle! Puke! Blood! Ugh! Uncle!

COP: Read him his rights, O'Reiley! Up against the wall! Spread yer legs!

O'REILEY: You have the right to remain——

COP: Kick!

CRIMINAL: Yiiiiiii!

(Blackout)

FIRST INTERMISSION

STAGE MANAGER: House lights. Intermission. Push. Smoke. Phonecall. Drink. Pee. Smoke. Push. Lobby Lights: on/off/on/off. Excuse me. Excuse me. Curtain up.

ACT TWO/Scene One

STAGE MANAGER: Act Two. Scene One. Thirteen years later. Court of Appeals:

(CRIMINAL *plays* Chopsticks *on the piano*.)

JURY FOREMAN: The juro findso defendo not guilto by reasoning of insanitary confinement.

ACT TWO/Scene Two

STAGE MANAGER: Scene Two. Thirteen times three: 39 years earlier. South Philadelphia Maternity Ward:

FATHER: Push! Push!

MOTHER: Ughhh! Ughhh!

INFANT CRIMINAL: Waaaa! Waaaa!

(FATHER *slaps* INFANT CRIMINAL. MOTHER *slaps* FATHER. *All slap each other excessively.*)

ACT TWO/Scene Three

STAGE MANAGER: Scene Three. Thirteen years after the thirteenth trial. Parole board hearing:

SHRINK: The patient manifests a dogphobia not unlike that attributed to Son of Sam Sequel in my exclusive *National Star* study, Volume 13, Number 3. We have talked at length in my office about the various merits of Dalmations vs. Irish Setters as Seeing Eye Dogs, as well as the theoretical ease in decapitating either species. The patient does wish to address the Board.

PAROLE BOARD: Speak! Speak! Speak! Speak!

CRIMINAL: Everybody, hurt the dogs!

(*He howls an ultra-high-pitched scream. Blackout.*)

SECOND INTERMISSION

STAGE MANAGER: House lights. Intermission. Push. Smoke. Pee. Wanna leave? Whataya think? Drink. Drink. Coffee. Stiffer drink. On/off/on/off. Excuse me. Excuse me. Curtain up.

ACT THREE/Scene One

STAGE MANAGER: Act Three. Scene One. The thirteenth dimension. Inside the minds of each character:

SPINNING ACTRESS: The dead woman: ooooooooooooooo . . . (*Continues*)

SPINNING ACTRESS: The three-month husband: woe, oh, woe, oh, woe . . . (*Continues*)

ANOTHER SPINNING ACTOR: The wealthy ex: (*Jingles change in his pocket and continues.*)

ANOTHER SPINNING ACTOR: The better-looking ex: fuck me — fuck me — fuck me — fuck me . . . (*Continues*)

ANOTHER SPINNING ACTOR: The hair stylist: (*Sniffs and continues.*)

ANOTHER SPINNING ACTOR: The after-hours bouncer: (*Punches fist into hand, bounces, and continues.*)

MANY SPINNING ACTRESSES: The Mah Jongg players: yadda-yadda-yadda-yadda . . . (*Continue*)

SPINNING COP: The cop: Bang! Bang! Bang! Bang! . . . (*Continues*)

SPINNING CRIMINAL: The criminal: Everybody, hurt the dogs! (*High-pitch scream and continues.*)

TWO SPINNING PARENTS: The parents: (*Slap each other and continue.*)

SPINNING SHRINK: The shrink: Another Jew — Another book, Another Jew — Another book . . . (*Continues*)

SPINNING STAGE MANAGER: The stage manager: Equity — Equity — Equity — Equity . . . (*Continues. Blackout.*)

ACT THREE/Scene Two

STAGE MANAGER: Scene Two. Thirteen seconds before the Act One, Scene One Full-Moon Friday murder Pre-Mah Jongg game chatter:

ACTRESS: Did you try the Devil's Food Cake?

ANOTHER ACTRESS: I'm on a diet.

FIRST ACTRESS: It's the Sweet and Low recipe.

THIRD ACTRESS: Who else can we call for a fourth?

SECOND ACTRESS: How's your snotty little niece, Shirley?

SHIRLEY (*First Actress*): All right, so let me call . . . Ring — Ring —— Ring — Ring . . .

SECOND ACTRESS: Isn't *TWILIGHT ZONE* on TV tonight?

THIRD ACTRESS: Life's too short for *TWILIGHT ZONE* reruns.

SHIRLEY: Ring — Ring —— Ring — Ring . . .

(*Blackout*)

DUAL ENCORE

STAGE MANAGER: Curtain call. Encore. Curtain down. Who broke the dressingroom mirror? Curtain up. Second Encore. (*In the dark*) Excuse me. Sorry! I said excuse me, get off my foot! On/off/on/off/ow! I hope your limo runs over a black cat on your way home from the theatre tonight! Taxi! Taxi! . . .

(*SOUND CUES: Car horn honks. Car crash. Cat.*)

(*END*)

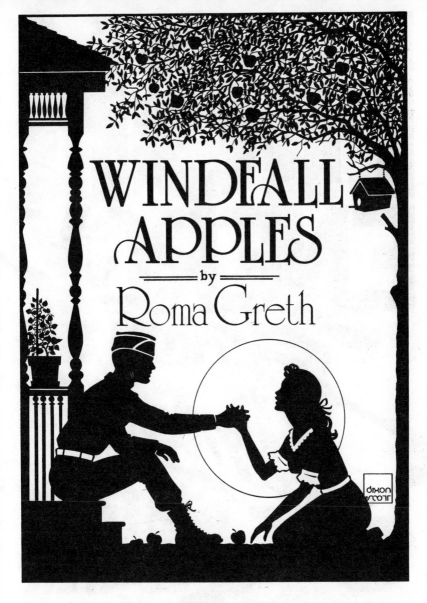

WINDFALL APPLES

by

Roma Greth

This gem of a play evokes the **days of youth and innocence** as our boys were being shipped off to World War II. This play workshopped at the **Eugene O'Neill Theater Center** in the summer of 1977, and then was produced in Manhattan at the IRT late in 1978. Three males, three females; single interior and exterior set.

HIGH ENERGY

MUSICALS

FROM THE

Omaha

MAGIC THEATER

This volume contains three of the dynamic shows created by members of the Omaha Magic Theatre: **Megan Terry**, Jo Ann Schmidman, Marianne de Pury, Lynn Herrick and John J. Sheehan. AMERICAN KING'S ENGLISH FOR QUEENS, RUNNING GAG, BABES IN THE BIGHOUSE are all shows that call for more females than males, and have simple flexible sets.

BATTERY

BY DANIEL THERRIAULT

Electricity is the central metaphor and an expressive image for this unusual love story set in an electrical workshop. This young playwright has been compared to Sam Shepard and David Mamet for his superb use of language. Two males, one female; single interior set.

MOLLY BAILEY'S TRAVELING FAMILY CIRCUS

featuring

SCENES FROM THE LIFE OF MOTHER JONES

BY MEGAN TERRY & JOANN METCALF

A musical presentation of magical and possible events in the lives of two women born in the last century. A minimum of three males and four females, though it can be expanded to accommodate a great number; may be done with simple fluid staging. A piano vocal score is available for perusal or rental.

SAGA

by Kelly Hamilton

This wonderful musical is a history of America's pioneers as they push their way across the country. A minimum of eight males and eight females are necessary, and the show can be expanded to use many more actors. Settings can be fluid and simple or elaborate. A piano vocal score is available for perusal or rental.

One Acts ~ And ~ Monologues ~ For ~ Women

BY ~ LUDMILLA BOLLOW

These haunting plays mark the arrival of a new voice in the American Theater. This volume consists of two thirty to thirty-five minute monologues and a forty minute one-act for two women. All three call for simple interior sets.